Date Due

DEC 2 8 1973	NOV 1 8 1991
MAY 4 1974	JAN 2 4 1995
JUN - 7 1974	OCT 2 0 '96
FEB 3 - 1977	
APR 1 4 1977	

142036

j971   Kerr, D.
Ker   Canada: a visual
          history.

                              850

DEC 2 8 1973	P.L. Noon
MAY 4 1974	R. Stoves
JUN - 7 1974	Bay	NOV 1 8 1991
	1977 P Buswell 45029

142036

j971   Kerr, Donald Gordon Grady, 1913-   ed.
Ker   Canada: a visual history [by] D.G.G. Kerr
          and R.I.K. Davidson. Toronto, Nelson,
          1966.
          170 p. illus., maps.

          Includes bibliography.

          1. Canada - Hist. - Pictorial works.
       I. Davidson, R   I   K   24757
      II. Title.   20310
                                       LC

Canada A VISUAL HISTORY

for Martha Elaine and Jess

D.G.G. KERR and R.I.K. DAVIDSON

Canada A VISUAL HISTORY

Toronto: Thomas Nelson & Sons (Canada) Limited

©1966 Thomas Nelson & Sons (Canada) Limited

Printed in Canada by The Bryant Press Limited

SBN   176   35005   5

CONTENTS

1

2

PREFACE

In the course of editing *A Historical Atlas of Canada*, it occurred to me that a companion volume of pictures would help round out the visual presentation of Canadian history that I was attempting. The present work is the result. The text and visual materials are closely associated as was the case with the *Atlas*, but in subject matter the two volumes differ considerably for the obvious reason that topics best treated on maps cannot always be illustrated pictorially and *vice versa*. Contrary to the policy adopted by C. W. Jefferys in his well-known and extremely useful books, contemporary sources — drawings, paintings, manuscripts, and photographs — have been used almost exclusively.

My part of the joint task of editing this volume has been to prepare the outline in detail, search out pictures to illustrate it, and when a selection from these had been made and pages laid out by R. I. K. Davidson, write the accompanying text. In fact, however, because of our long friendship and the experience we gained in working together during the compilation of the *Atlas*, our collaboration at all stages has been much closer than this would indicate.

We are immensely grateful to archives and individuals who have supplied photographs and given permission for their use; their names are given on pages 163 and 164. We would acknowledge too our indebtedness to all those who have given us much needed advice and particularly to Mr. Lucien Brault, whose help was of special value during the early stages of research.

July 1, 1966   D. G. G. KERR

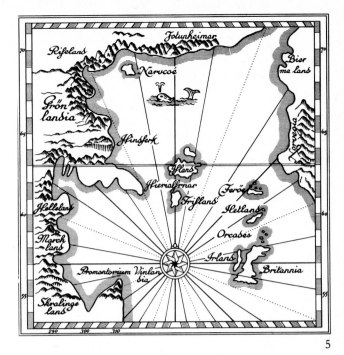

5

4

3

1. EARLY ARRIVALS IN NORTH AMERICA

1. Eskimo killing seal
2. Eskimo walking
3. Tools used by early Eskimo on Banks Island
4. Skin-covered boat used by natives to cross Bering Strait
5. Map by Sigurdus Stephanius, 1570

It has long been assumed that the Indians and Eskimo crossed Bering Strait from Asia in prehistoric times and during the course of many hundreds of years spread out from Alaska to various parts of North and South America. Until recently, this assumption was supported mainly by knowledge of how easily the Strait could be crossed even by natives in quite primitive boats. Now definite evidence of these early migrations has been uncovered by archeological examination of ancient camp sites such as the one on Banks Island where 4000-year-old Eskimo tools were found in the summer of 1965.

Coming from the opposite direction, the first Europeans to approach North America seem to have been the Vikings in the late tenth or early eleventh century. Knowledge of this has been rather sketchy—vaguely worded accounts in the Norse sagas, a map drawn long afterwards by Stephanius, relics found in various parts of North America and later proved to be fraudulent. Controversy rather than significant additional information has been the result of most of the many books written on the subject. In a different category seem to be a recently discovered Vinland Map said to date from about 1440 and excavations undertaken

in the early 1960's by Helge Ingstad at L'Anse au Meadow in Newfoundland. At this latter site, the footings of nine buildings were located along with charred wood and other relics shown by radiocarbon dating to belong to the Viking period.

1

3

1

2

A. The Habit of ye Fishermen. B. The Line. C. The manner of Fishing. D. The Dressers of ye Fish. E. The Trough into which they throw ye Cod when Dressed. F. Salt Boxes. G. The manner of Carrying ye Cod. H. The Cleansing ye Cod. I. A Press to extract ye Oyl from ye Cod Livers. K. Casks to receive ye Water and Blood that comes from ye Livers. L. Another Cask to receive ye Oyl. M. The manner of Drying ye Cod.

More significant than the Viking voyages in making Canada known to Europeans were those of John Cabot in 1497 and of other explorers in the next few years from England, Portugal, Spain, and France. Like Columbus before them, all had as their main purpose the discovery of a sea route westwards to the fabled riches of China and Japan. What were found instead were the abundant fisheries of the Grand Banks and the Gulf of St. Lawrence. Fishermen from western Europe were soon making their way across to these in their small boats each summer as they have continued to do ever since. By the time of Jacques Cartier's first voyage in 1534, the Newfoundland cod fisheries had begun their long and, until recently, almost unchanging history.

Cartier made three voyages to the St. Lawrence in the 1530's and '40's but failed in his attempt either to discover wealth in North America or a way through to that of China. His achievements, nevertheless, were of lasting importance. He had found a major entry to the North American continent and his writings served to arouse interest in it. His *Bref récit*, as the title began, of his second and most important voyage was printed in Paris in 1545. The account of his first voyage, strangely enough, did not appear until 1556, the year before his death, and then in an Italian translation by Giovanni Ramusio. This in turn was translated into English in 1580 and back into French in 1598 just in time to play its part in attracting to the St. Lawrence the attention of a new generation of Frenchmen, the generation that included Champlain.

The discovery of Hudson Bay, the other main Canadian gateway to the continent, also arose from the continuing search for a route to the orient. The possibility that this might be found in a passage north of the North American continent became of particular in-

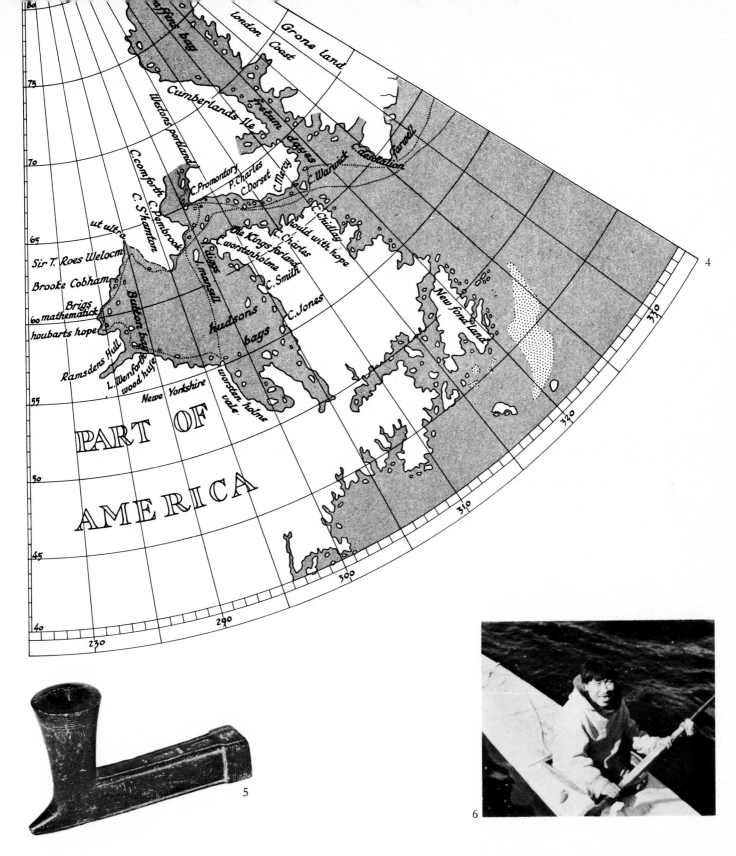

Map labels (clockwise, as legible): London Coast, Grone land, Cumberlands Ile, Fretum dauies, C.destration, C.farewell, Westons portland, C.comfort, C.Promontory, P.Charles, C.Dorset, C.Mercy, C.Warwick, C.Pembroke, C.S'hamton, ut ultra, old Kings forland, C.Charles, gould with hope, Chidlay, Sir T. Roes Welcom, Diggs, C.worstenholme, C.Smith, Brooke Cobham, I.mansell, C.Jones, Brigs mathematick, Buttons bay, houbarts hope, Hudsons bays, New fond land, Ramsdens Hull, L.Wenford wood huse, Newe Yorkshire, worsten holme vale

PART OF AMERICA

5

6

terest in England in the second half of the sixteenth century. In 1576 and for the next two years in succession, Martin Frobisher sought such a passage unsuccessfully. His achievement, however, like that of Cartier, was to arouse interest in the region and its strange inhabitants, the Eskimo. One of these in a kayak he had plucked "with main force, boate and al . . . out of the Sea" and carried off to exhibit in England—where the poor man died of a cold!

The most important of these northern voyages was that of Henry Hudson who in the *Discovery* in 1610 made his way through the difficult strait that now bears his name and reached open waters beyond. There, as is well known, his man mutinied and set him adrift to vanish from history. The story, eventually extracted from the mutineers, on their return home, fired men's imaginations, not only because of its drama, but because of the hope it held out that at last the open waters of the Pacific had been reached by a north-west passage. In the years that followed a number of voyages, based on this hope, were made, four of them in the veteran *Discovery* and all but one by Englishmen. By 1635 when Luke "North West" Foxe published his account of

his voyage of four years before along with his famous map, it was clear that Hudson had merely entered a great bay beyond which lay more ice and land. For many years, interest in the north-west passage ceased.

3

1
2

The re-awakening of French interest in North America at the beginning of the seventeenth century occurred because the steadily growing value of the fur trade coincided with a desire on the part of the king, Henry IV, once free of civil war at home, to emulate Spain's dazzling success overseas. It became his practice to grant a monopoly of the fur trade in return for promotion of settlement. Fur trade and settlement along with the Christianizing of the Indians were to be the key factors throughout the history of New France.

The central role in the events of the period was played by one of the most remarkable men in Canadian history, Samuel de Champlain. About 30 when he made his first voyage to the St. Lawrence in 1603, Champlain spent the next four years exploring the Bay of Fundy and the Atlantic coast to the south of it and helping establish a "habitation" or fur trading post first on Dochet Island in the St. Croix River and, when that proved unsatisfactory, at Port Royal in what is now the rich Annapolis valley. In 1608 as lieutenant of the current monopolist De Monts, he re-entered the St. Lawrence and chose the site of Quebec as a base for fur trading and for further explorations which he hoped might even lead to discovery of a passage to China.

Champlain's personal explorations in the years that followed were supplemented by information he received from the Indians and early missionaries and from young Frenchmen he sent out to live among the Indians primarily to encourage the latter to bring their furs down each spring to the St. Lawrence. His final great map of 1632 shows how much accurate information he had been able to collect despite the need to rely on the simple

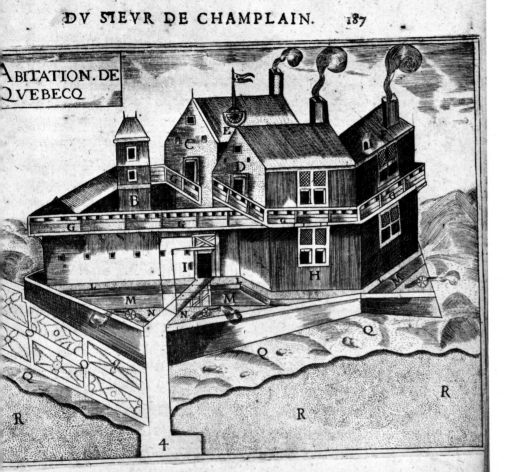

ABITATION.DE QVEBECQ

A Le magazin.
B Colombier.
C Corps de logis où font nos armes,& pour loger les ouuriers.
D Autre corps de logis pour les ouuriers.
E Cadran.
F Autre corps de logis où est la forge, & artifans logés.
G Galleries tout au tour des

logemens.
H Logis du sieur de Champlain.
I La porte de l'habitation, où il y a Pont-leuis
L Promenoir autour de l'habitation contenant 10. pieds de large iufques fur le bort du fossé.
M Fossés tout autour de l'habitation.

N Plattes formes, en façon de tenailles pour mettre le canon.
O Iardin du fieur de Champlain.
P La cuisine.
Q Place deuant l'habitation sur le bort de la riuiere.
R La grande riuiere de sainct Lorens.

A a ij

3

4

5

Champlain—

instruments of the time such as the astrolabe. It shows too his skill as a geographer in putting it all together and obtaining a surprisingly correct impression of the main waterways of the northeastern part of the continent. That Champlain was less successful as a colonizer was the fault of the successive monopolists for whom he worked. Interested only in profits from the fur trade, they did little to fulfil their obligation to support settlement. And when prospects finally brightened with the formation of the large Company of One Hundred Associates in 1627, war with England

intervened disastrously.

England had never accepted France's claims to the northern part of the continent. In 1613 Samuel Argall from Virginia had burned the "habitation" at Port Royal and in 1621 James I granted what he called "Nova Scotia" to Sir William Alexander. In 1628 after formal war between England and France had broken out, David Kirke led an expedition into the St. Lawrence to seize French shipping. The following winter Champlain and his tiny settlement at Quebec—it never had more than 50 or 60 year-round inhabitants at this time—

barely survived and by spring everyone was reduced to digging for edible roots in the woods. When Kirke appeared again in 1629 there was no alternative but to surrender.

After peace was made and the St. Lawrence region and Acadia restored to France, Champlain returned to spend his last years in Quebec under more hopeful circumstances. When he died there in 1635, the colony he had striven so hard to found was beginning at last to emerge from its troubled and prolonged infancy.

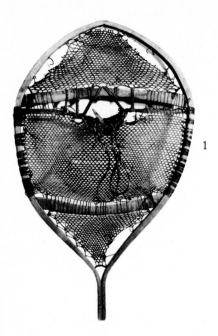

1

2

4. THE INDIANS AND THE FUR TRADE

1. Montagnais snowshoe
2. Wampum belt of 1200 purple beads and 72 white ones, 1640
3. Montagnais Indian making birch-bark canoe
4. Indian making birch-bark canoe at Murray Bay, P.Q.
5. Beavers at work. From Moll Map of 1713
6. Fur-trade goods recovered by skin-diver from French River

3   4

Of the several dramatic encounters that took place between the Indian and white cultures while the latter was becoming dominant in North America, only those connected with Mexico and the opening of the American and Canadian West compare in significance with that which occurred during the creation of France's great seventeenth and eighteenth century fur-trading empire based on the St. Lawrence. The French experience differed in one important respect from the others. The Indians they were in contact with had neither the gold and silver of Mexico nor rich land needed for settlement. Simple robbery was

not, therefore, the French objective. Instead, a close and co-operative association was wanted partly out of a sincere Christian desire to save Indian souls, partly because active Indian participation was needed in the fur trade.

Fur, and in particular that of the beaver, was of fundamental importance in the economy of New France. The special value of the beaver lay in the fact that its underfur contained numerous microscopic barbs giving it the matting quality required for making high-grade felt. With the export of beaver skins from the Saguenay and the St. Lawrence becoming substantial in the early seventeenth

century, beaver-felt hats took on a new popularity in France and the rest of Western Europe. At that time, beavers were still numerous. Their habit of living in colonies, however, and building log lodges and dams—not quite as imagined by Moll—made them extremely vulnerable to hunters armed with guns and metal knives and hatchets. Their virtual extermination in ever widening circles out from the French posts was bound to result. By the end of the French régime the La Vérendrye's were seeking new hunting grounds far to the west of the Great Lakes.

Allies of the French in their search for furs

The Cataract of NIAGARA, some make this water Fall to be half a League while others reckon it no more than a hundred Fathom.

A View of y^e Industry of y^e Beavers of Canada in making Dams to stop y^e Course of à Rivulet, in order to form a great Lake, about wch they build their Habitations. To Effect this: they fell large Trees with their Teeth, in such a manner as to make them come Crofs ye Rivulet, to lay ye foundation of y^e Dam: they make Mortar, work up, and finish y^e whole with great order and wonderfull Dexterity. The Beavers have two Doors to their Lodges, one to the water and the other to the Land side. According to y^e French Accounts.

5

6

were the Montagnais of the Saguenay region and other Algonkian tribes of the Laurentian forests as far west as the Chippewas and the Ojibwas north of Lake Superior. These, with their knowledge of the forests and the ways of animals, their birch-bark canoes in summer and snowshoes in winter, and the metals pots, hatchets, knives and other trade goods obtained from the French, were well equipped for the nomadic life of hunters which they had always lived. The more advanced semi-agricultural Hurons in the fertile land south of Georgian Bay became middlemen in the trade, purchasing furs from the more distant tribes of the north and west and bringing them down the Ottawa to the French settlements on the St. Lawrence. Their principal enemy, and that of the French, was the Iroquois confederacy living south of Lake Ontario. Similar to the Hurons in language and economy, the Iroquois eventually became stronger partly because of their more advanced political organization which was reinforced annually by means of federal council meetings at Onondaga. Here wampum belts with special combinations of light and dark beads served to remind orators of agreements reached in the past and great deeds accomplished. A second advantage of the Iroquois was their strategic location between the Dutch or English to the south and the French to the north. This enabled them to play off one against the other and gather the strength necessary to destroy their Huron, and very nearly their French, rivals and attempt to take over the whole fur trade themselves and funnel it down the Hudson River.

7

5. THE MISSIONARIES AND THE INDIANS

1. Title page of the *Relation* for 1636
2. Martyrdoms of Gabriel Lalemant, Jean de Brébeuf, and others. From Du Creux, *Historiæ Canadensis* (Paris, 1664)
3. Signature of Brébeuf
4. Portrait of Marie de l'Incarnation. From *La Vie de Marie de l'Incarnation*, edited by her son (Paris, 1677)
5. Huron log house at Ste. Marie during reconstruction

2

1

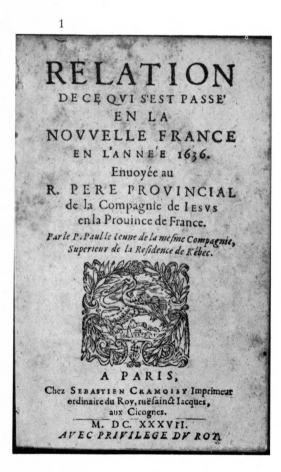

RELATION
DE CE QVI S'EST PASSE'
EN LA
NOVVELLE FRANCE
EN L'ANNE'E 1636.
Enuoyée au
R. PERE PROVINCIAL
de la Compagnie de Iesvs
en la Prouince de France.

Par le P. Paul le ieune de la mesme Compagnie,
Superieur de la Residence de Kébec.

A PARIS,
Chez Sebastien Cramoisy Imprimeur
ordinaire du Roy, ruë sainct Iacques,
aux Cicognes.
M. DC. XXXVII.
AVEC PRIVILEGE DV ROY.

3

Joannes de Brebeuf soc Ies

Frenchmen in the early seventeenth century regarded New France as more than just a fur-trading post adjacent to the Newfoundland fisheries. They were interested in it as well as a centre from which missionary endeavours could radiate out to the savage tribes of North America and bring them the blessings of Christianity. In an intensely religious age, this aspect of the colony seemed of real importance and resulted in considerable support from France that otherwise would not have been given—support without which the colony might well have succumbed along with

the Huron nation during the dark days of Iroquois attack in the 1640's and '50's.

Early missionary efforts such as those of the Jesuits Biard and Massé in Acadia or Recollets like Le Caron in Huronia were unsuccessful. The task was overwhelmingly great. A more ambitious attempt begun by the Jesuits in 1625 was interrupted when Kirke's attack ended all French activity in 1629. A fresh start came in 1632 when Father Le Jeune landed at Quebec as Superior General of a new Jesuit mission in Canada. He brought with him only one other priest and a lay brother

but the following year several others including Jean de Brébeuf arrived and work on a considerable scale could begin.

The obvious Jesuit strategy seemed to be to concentrate their main effort on the populous and sedentary Hurons already closely associated with the French in the fur trade. Brébeuf who had spent the years from 1626 to 1629 among them was chosen to found what was expected to become a substantial mission. Accordingly, in 1634 he and two other priests accompanied a party of Indians on the strenuous 800-mile journey to Huronia. In the years that

4

5

followed, others were added to their number, almost a dozen missions were established, and a central mission fort was built at Ste. Marie. By 1645 when the total white population of New France had barely reached 250, that of Ste. Marie was 58, 22 of them soldiers.

Beginning with his voyage out in 1632, Father Le Jeune made it a practice to send back to France for publication annual reports or *Relations* of missionary activity. These were continued by his successors until 1673 and aroused widespread interest in the colony throughout France. The *Relation* of 1636 has a special value in that the whole of the second half of it is a detailed report by Brébeuf on Huronia. Among others, Marie de l'Incarnation, one of the most remarkable women in Canadian history, was inspired by the *Relation* to come to New France where she became the first missionary nun and foundress of the Canadian branch of the Ursuline Order.

Although much was accomplished by what became quite a large group of completely devoted men and women, many of whom were unusually gifted, the hardships were great and the results disappointing. Disastrous epidemics of influenza and smallpox in the 1630's reduced the Huron population in a few years from 30,000 to 12,000 and were blamed on the "black robes." Conversions except among the elderly and dying were slow to come. And in the end Iroquois attacks in 1648 and 1649 completely destroyed the Hurons as a nation. Brébeuf after almost 28 years among them met martyrdom, as did four of his colleagues. The work of missions was to continue among other tribes, even the Iroquois, but hopes would never again be as high.

1

Paul de Chomedey. De maisonneufue

2

3

4

The wave of interest in Canadian missions that had brought the Jesuits to Quebec and Huronia was responsible also for the founding of Montreal. Indeed, much of the inspiration that lay behind both Montreal and the Jesuit missions seems to have centred around the same Jesuit college at La Flèche in northwestern France. There Paul Le Jeune and several of the other great missionaries of New France listened in their youth to Father Massé's account of his experiences in Acadia. There Jérôme Le Royer de La Dauversière, a pupil of the college before becoming a local tax collector, hardly needed the supernatural revelation he is said to have had to become interested in founding a mission city on the Canadian frontier. A Jesuit of the college put him in touch with his co-founder, the founder of the Sulpicians, Jean Jacques Olier. Before long the Société de Notre Dame de Montréal was in being and had acquired seigneurial rights to the island. Paul de Chomedey de Maisonneuve, who was to be the leader of the colonists, and Jeanne Mance, their bursar and later nurse, were brought into the group shortly by acquaintances with La Flèche connections.

The early years of Montreal from its founding in 1642 until well after Maisonneuve's departure in 1665 and Jeanne Mance's death in 1673 were years of hardship and uncertainty. On several occasions, Iroquois raids seemed likely to bring about either the distruction or the abandonment of the colony. Even after Maisonneuve managed to recruit over 100 new soldier-settlers in 1653, the situation continued to deteriorate. Only good fortune and the brave action by Dollard and his 16 companions at the Long Sault in 1660 averted a large-scale attack which might have proved overwhelming. Some improvement took place gradually in the years that followed,

6

7

5

but when the wars with England opened with the Lachine massacre in 1689 a new period of danger was to begin.

Despite all dangers and the transformation of Montreal before the end of the century into the leading fur-trading centre, the mission purpose behind its founding was not forgotten. Jeanne Mance's Hôtel Dieu was begun in 1644 and became the early town's most impressive building caring for Indians and French alike. The first Gentleman of the Order of St. Sulpice arrived in 1657 and in 1663 the Order took over seigneurial rights from the Société de Montréal now rapidly being reduced by

death. In the 1670's the first Notre Dame was built and beside it rose the old Sulpician Seminary with Montreal's earliest public clock on its facade. Out of town, on the lower slopes of the mountain, the Sulpicians began to gather Indian converts around their Fort des Messieurs, rebuilt in stone in the 1690's by Abbé Vachon de Belmont.

Supplementing the work of Sulpicians such as Vachon among the boys was that of Marguerite Bourgeois among the girls both Indian and French. From the time of her arrival in 1653, until her death in 1700, she displayed remarkable teaching and administrative ability

especially in connection with the founding of her Congrégation de Notre Dame, an order of uncloistered teaching nuns that has since spread widely through North America. She established a number of small schools in which members of the order taught, one in a tower of Vachon's fort, another as far away as Ste. Famille on the Island of Orleans. The Ferme St. Gabriel on Point St. Charles which she acquired and where she erected a fine stone house in 1698, has remained the "home farm" of the order.

1

2

3

4

5

By a fortunate coincidence, in the early 1660's when New France was being dragged down to the point of collapse by Iroquois attacks, Louis XIV and his great minister Colbert were ready for the first time to give it their serious attention and support. They took energetic steps over the next decade to re-organize the government, carry the war to the Iroquois, bring out new settlers, and generally develop the colony as part of an invigorated French mercantile empire. In-terest at this high level was not long sustained, however, and a century later at the end of the last of a long series of wars with Britain,

Louis's successor was obliged to sign away his rights to New France altogether. During the intervening generations and despite the fre-quent warfare, there had been created on the banks of the St. Lawrence a French-Canadian society that had a distinctive character of its own and that was sufficiently firmly entrenched to withstand the shock of conquest and alien rule.

That this had been achieved was owing in no small part to the firm foundations laid by Laval on the spiritual side and by Talon on the economic. Laval, part of whose early training had been at La Flèche, arrived at

Quebec first in 1659 as Apostolic Vicar and Bishop of Petraea. He became the first Bishop of Quebec on the creation of that see in 1674. A man of aristocratic birth and temper-ament, he played an important role in govern-ment as a member of the Sovereign Council and fought vigorously from time to time with governors and intendants especially against the sale of liquor to the Indians. His major contributions were the organization of a parish clergy and the founding of the Quebec Seminary where they and others could be trained. He retired in 1688 on account of ill-health but remained on in his beloved

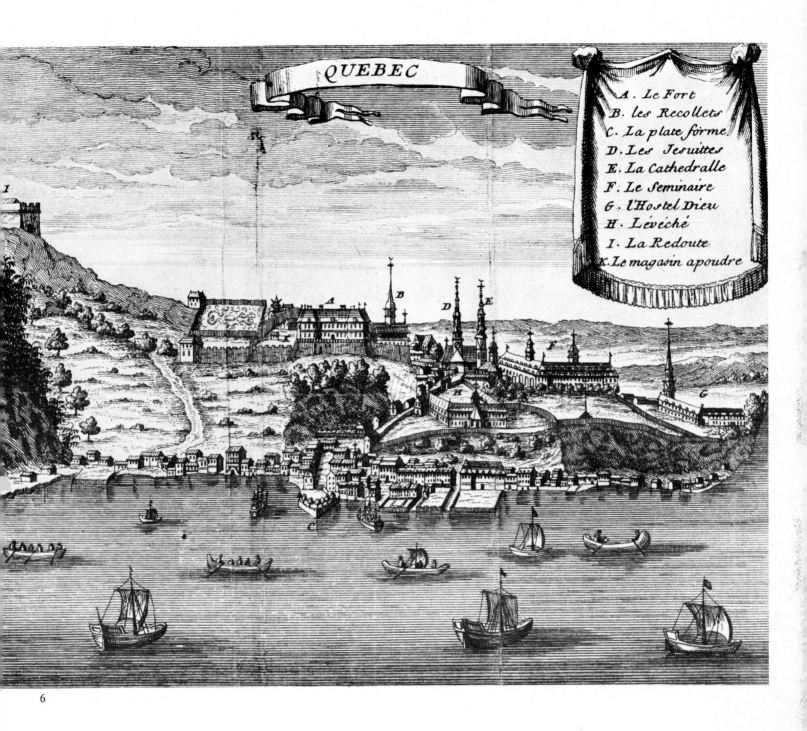

Seminary until his death in 1708.

Talon's time in Canada was much shorter, three years beginning in 1665 and two more after a two-year interval in France. As Intendant of Justice, Police, and Finance, Talon was responsible for the whole civil administration of the colony, leaving military and Indian affairs to the governor. His particular task was to promote settlement and build up the colony's economy in accordance with his instructions from the king. This he proceeded to undertake with great energy and imagination. By encouraging immigration, early marriages, and a high birth rate, he doubled the population, increasing it to over 7500 by the time of his departure. He promoted the clearing of land and the raising not only of grain and vegetables but of hemp for the shipbuilding industry he was trying to establish, hops for a brewery, and flax for spinning and weaving. Lumbering and fishing were given substantial aid with a view to developing trade with the West Indies. The fur trade was not neglected and assistance was given for further exploration around the Great Lakes and down the Mississippi. Some of the things he attempted collapsed when his energetic support was withdrawn. A number of his successors were able men however—one had the imagination to take care of the perennial shortage of currency by inventing card money—and gradually during the eighteenth century Quebec, Montreal, and Three Rivers developed into thriving, well-built towns and the countryside all along the St. Lawrence and Richelieu rivers came to enjoy modest prosperity.

1

2

3

7. THE CHARACTER OF NEW FRANCE.
II, THE EIGHTEENTH CENTURY

1. Kneeling Angel. By François Nöel Lavasseur (1705-1794)
2. Outdoor oven
3. Church at Ste. Famille, Island of Orleans
4. Dog cart
5. Forges of St. Maurice. By J. Bouchette, Jr.
6. St. Luke with ox. By Paul Jourdain *dit* Labrosse (1697-1773)
7. Old Presbytery at Batiscan
8. Stone windmill

Peter Kalm, the well-known Swedish botanist, visited New France in 1749 while on an extensive North American tour. His account shows that life there had already taken on distinctive characteristics some of which would persist almost unchanged until well into the twentieth century. His attention was attracted, for example, as has been that of succeeding generations of tourists, by outdoor bake ovens and the dogs used as "poor man's horses." Of the latter he wrote: " . . . they use their dogs to fetch water out of the river. I saw two great dogs today attached to a little

cart, one before the other. . . . In the cart was a barrel. The dogs were directed by a boy. . . . Sometimes they put one dog before the water cart. . . . Almost all the wood, which the poorer people in this country fetch out of the woods in winter, is drawn by dogs, which have therefore got the name of 'the poor man's horse.'"

Travelling through the countryside Kalm noted that "it could really be called a village, beginning at Montreal and ending at Quebec . . . for the farmhouses are never above five arpents, and sometimes but three apart, a few places excepted." The houses were

"generally built of stone" and had glass in the windows except in the more remote regions where paper might be used. Nearby, there might be a windmill also of stone "with a roof of boards which together with its wings could be turned to the wind." Kalm paid a special visit to the recently opened iron forges on the St. Maurice where they "cast cannon and mortars . . . of different sizes, iron stoves which were used all over Canada, kettles, etc.".

Church steeples have long been the most characteristic landmarks of French Canada.

8

5

6

7

4

Most of the early parish churches had been of frame construction but by the 1730's and '40's these were falling into ruins and were being replaced by fine stone buildings. Typical was the church at Sault au Récollet where the stone for the new building was ready on the site when Kalm visited it. Ste. Famille on the other hand was one of the few to be built originally in stone in 1669 when stone masons were still comparatively rare in the colony. The early structure had been replaced shortly before Kalm's time by the building that still stands with its five unusual niches in the façade.

The side towers and the three belfries were to be early nineteenth century additions.

Wood carving had become firmly established in the eighteenth century as the favourite form of French-Canadian art. The best of the carvers at Quebec, the leading centre because of its size and importance, were not simple folk craftsmen. From the later seventeenth century, Laval's Seminary had been providing expert training in the arts and crafts under such masters as Jacques le Blond de La Tour brought out from France. Wood carving was especially popular because of its

use in the interior decoration of churches and other religious establishments. Outstanding in Quebec were the Lavasseurs, father, two sons, and a cousin, all born and trained in New France and all much in demand in that church-building age. Montreal, still little more than a mission and fur-trading outpost, had less work for the sculptor. Most well-known there was Paul Jourdain *dit* Labrosse, probably born and trained in France and founder of a family of sculptors who continued to work in Montreal on into the nineteenth century.

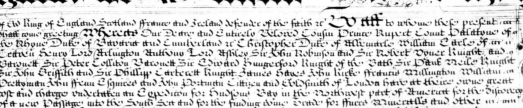

1

8. TROUBLE ON THE PERIMETER

1. Hudson's Bay Company Charter, May, 1670

2. Fort Lawrence, Chignecto, 1755. By Capt. J. Hamilton of the 40th Regiment

3. Wreck of D'Iberville's *Pelican* in Hudson Bay. In Bacqueville de la Potherie, *Histoire de l'Amérique septentrionale* (Paris, 1722)

4. Grenadier of the Carignan-Salière Regiment, 1665. By H. Beau

5. Frontenac's signature

6. Fort Chambly

7. Ruins of Fort Prince of Wales

8. Halifax, 1759. By Richard Short

2

An account of modestly prosperous settlements in the St. Lawrence valley and in parts of Acadia and of a widespread fur empire in the interior does not tell the whole story of New France. Its setting within the North American continent must be considered as well. To the south and east were English rivals in New England and after 1664 in New York when that colony was acquired from the Dutch. To the southwest were the Iroquois, associated with the English in the fur trade. To the north, after it received its charter in 1670, was the English Hudson's Bay Company. In Newfoundland, English and French had long occupied separate sections of the coastline in uneasy rivalry. Trouble along such a perimeter was bound to be almost continuous.

The early Iroquois attacks that had threatened to overwhelm the colony had been brought to an end as a result of Louis XIV's decision to send out a full regiment, the Carignan-Salières, in 1665. Two campaigns the following year into the Iroquois country, whatever their military failings, had had the desired psychological effect and had brought peace. That this did not last very long was primarily because of the natural rivalry certain to develop between the St. Lawrence as one of the great fur-trading outlets of the continent and the other two the Hudson River and Hudson Bay. The fact that these two were in English hands meant, of course, that much depended as well on the current relations between the two mother countries. When they were at peace troubles in North America would, as a rule, be confined to skirmishes and border incidents—blamed if at all possible on the Indians. When they were at war, fighting on quite a large scale could be expected.

The first of the long series of English-French wars broke out in 1689 and, with the exception of a five-year interval following the Treaty of Ryswick in 1697, fighting continued until 1713. Among the major events in North

16

5 Frontenac

America were Phipps' failure with a New England fleet to bluff Frontenac into the surrender of Quebec in 1690 and several stirring naval victories by D'Iberville in Hudson Bay. Characteristic of these latter was that of 1697 recorded by La Potherie, the fleet commissary, who was on board D'Iberville's *Pelican* at the time. While awaiting the rest of the French fleet the *Pelican* came unexpectantly upon three English warships, sank one, drove another off, and captured the third before herself going aground in the storm that had come up during the battle. Generally, throughout the war in North America victory was on the side of the French. It was

in Europe, however, that the outcome was decided by the armies of Marlborough and his allies. In the Treaty of Utrecht (1713) France surrendered all her claims to Hudson Bay, Newfoundland, and Acadia (Nova Scotia).

Disastrous losses of this sort provoked in the generation following Vauban the natural reaction of beginning immediately to fortify as heavily as possible what was left. Most vital was Cape Breton Island, the largest French island left in the narrow entrance to the St. Lawrence between what were now British Newfoundland and Nova Scotia. The ink was hardly dry at Utrecht before an advance

party from France had chosen a site for Louisbourg. Corruption and inefficiency made subsequent progress less rapid but a fortress of imposing dimensions was eventually erected. Other, less elaborate, stone fortresses were built to guard other approaches—Niagara, St. Frédéric, and Beauséjour—while existing fortifications at Chambly, Fort Frontenac, and Quebec were strengthened. English forts such as Fort Lawrence opposite Beauséjour were as a rule much weaker than their French counterparts. Fort Prince of Wales on Hudson Bay was the exception being, next to Quebec and Louisbourg, the strongest fortified place on the continent.

17

1

2

9. THE FALL OF LOUISBOURG AND QUEBEC

1. "A view of Louisbourg ... when that City was besieged in 1758." By Capt. Ince of the 35th Regiment

2. Notre-Dame de la Victoire, Quebec, after the siege. By Richard Short

3. Sketch of Wolfe by his second-in-command, Brig. George Townshend

4. Montcalm. Artist unknown

5. Montcalm's surrender letter

6. Death of Montcalm (detail). By Louis Joseph Watteau

7. Death of Wolfe (detail). By Benjamin West

The long-drawn-out struggle between the English and the French on the North American continent ended with the Seven Years' War and victory for the English. This war like its predecessors was fought on a broad front. During its later stages, when the English began to gain the upper hand, they continued to attack in the Ohio and Great Lakes region but concentrated their main effort on a two-pronged invasion up the Hudson-Champlain-Richelieu "warpath of nations"

towards Montreal and up the St. Lawrence towards Quebec. It was this latter effort that succeeded in breaking through the elaborately constructed French defences, capturing Louisbourg in 1758 and then Quebec in 1759.

At Quebec, the young, rather sickly British commander, Wolfe, who had won his first independent command by his dash and skill at Louisbourg, faced the older urbane and aristocratic Montcalm. After a long summer's siege, Wolfe made his daring and brilliantly executed landing above the city and was killed during the battle that followed on the Plains of Abraham. Montcalm, also mortally

3

4

6

5   7

wounded, was carried back into the city and had barely time to begin arrangements for its surrender before he too died. The drama of these events, together with their significance, aroused widespread interest on both sides of the Atlantic resulting in such wholly imaginary paintings as those by the American Benjamin West and the Frenchman Louis Joseph Watteau.

In sharp contrast to the West and Watteau paintings, are others sketched on the spot by Captain Ince of the 35th Regiment at Louisbourg and Richard Short, the purser on H.M.S. *Prince of Orange* at Quebec. Ince and Short as part of the regular military training given British officers in the eighteenth century had been taught topographical drawing and painting in water colour. Their pictures and those of other officers such as Hervey Smyth, Thomas Davies, and J. F. W. DesBarres, all of whom took part in the conquest, give us our earliest authentic views of Canadian scenes and cities.

Article 4.

Sa Majesté Très Chrétienne renonce à toutes les Pretensions, qu'Elle a formées ——— autrefois, ou pû former, à la Nouvelle Ecosse, ou l'Acadie, en toutes ses Parties, & la garantit toute entiere, & avec toutes ses Dependances au Roy de la Grande Bretagne. De plus, Sa Majesté Très Chretienne cede & garantit à Sa dite Majesté Britannique, en toute Proprieté, le Canada avec toutes ses Dependances, ainsi que l'Isle du Cap Breton, & toutes les autres Isles, & Côtes, dans le Golphe. & Fleuve St Laurent, & generalement tout ce qui depend des dits Pays, Terres, Isles, & Côtes, avec la Souveraineté, Proprieté, Possession, & tous Droits acquis par Traité, ou autrement, que le Roy Très Chrêtien et la Couronne de France ont eus jusqu'à present sur les dits Pays, Isles, Terres, Lieux, Côtes, & leurs Habitans; ainsi que le Roy Très Chretien cede & transporte le tout au dit Roy & à la Couronne de la Grande Bretagne, & cela de la maniere & dt la Forme la plus ample, sans Restriction, & sans qu'il soit libre de revenir sous aucun Pretexte contre cette Cession & Garantie, ni de troubler la Grande Bretagne dans les Possessions sus-mentionnées. De son Côté Sa Majesté Britannique convient d'accorder aux Habitans du Canada la Liberté de la ...

1

10. THE SURRENDER OF NEW FRANCE

1. Treaty of Paris, 1763, Article 4
2. A view of Montreal taken from St. Helen's Island in 1762. By Thomas Davies

The capture of Quebec was a great victory for the British but it did not end the war. Quebec remained in the possession of a British garrison under James Murray and some posts to the west were captured, but the main British army under Amherst was still making slow progress up Lake Champlain when winter set in, leaving Montreal and most of the rest of the country still in French hands. Energetic efforts by the new French commander, François Gaston Lévis, resulted in the patching together of a considerable force of French regulars and militia by spring giving some grounds for thinking that it might be possible to recapture Quebec. Indeed Lévis' attempt to do so in April 1760 very nearly succeeded. The British were driven back into the city after a sharp engagement at Ste. Foy and only the arrival of a British instead of a French fleet a week or so later forced Lévis to abandon the seige and return once again to Montreal.

There, without reinforcements and beset by British armies converging from three directions, the situation was hopeless. The capitulation of New France took place accordingly in Montreal on September 9, 1760. Military rule was established under Murray at Quebec, General Thomas Gage at Montreal, and

Colonel Ralph Burton and later Colonel Frederick Haldimand at Three Rivers. Normal conditions were soon restored and what administration was needed was conducted through the local French authorities as far as possible. Finally, in 1763 when the fighting had ended in Europe as well, the fourth article of the Treaty of Paris ceded all of New France to Britain.

Lieutenant Thomas Davies had been one of the officers in Amherst's army that advanced on Montreal from the west in 1760. He appears to have spent the next two years with the occupying troops there before being transferred to New York and going on eventually to a distinguished military career ending with the rank of lieutenant general. Davies is looked upon as probably the best of the topographical artists serving with the British armed forces in Canada at that time particularly for his ability, as R. H. Hubbard has put it, "to express the inner mystery of a scene." His idyllic view of Montreal during the period of military occupation suggests the peaceful relationship that had been established between the former enemies and the general confidence that in North America at least the long era of warfare had finally ended.

1

3

2

11. EARLY ENGLISH-FRENCH RELATIONS

1. Quebec after the siege, 1759. By Richard Short

2. Quebec in 1789. By Thomas Davies

3. Governor James Murray

4. Jean Olivier Briand, Bishop of Quebec, 1766-84

5. Major General Sir Guy Carleton, Lord Dorchester

6. Quebec *Gazette*, June 6, 1799

Early relationships between English and French were on the whole good. Credit for this belongs in no small measure to James Murray who went on from being military governor of the Quebec District to become the first civil governor of the whole colony from 1764 to 1766. During his time the rebuilding of the heavily bombarded city began, the bilingual Quebec *Gazette*, Canada's second newspaper, was founded, and arrangements were made to get around the difficulty of appointing a new bishop of Quebec. The former bishop, Pontbriand, had died shortly before the capitulation of Montreal. It took

six years and all of Murray's tactical skill to secure the appointment of an officially recognized successor—and it was remarkable that he succeeded at all at a time when anti-Catholic sentiment was running high in England and Roman Catholics were still denied the right to hold public office anywhere in the British Empire. Briand, Murray's own choice for the appointment, was wise and conciliatory and did much over the years to smooth relations between the two groups.

Murray was recalled in 1766 to face charges of being overly sympathetic to the French and unfair to the small English minor-

4

5

6

NUM. 1779.

THE QUEBEC GAZETTE.

LA GAZETTE DE QUEBEC.

THURSDAY, 6 JUNE 1799.

JEUDI, LE 6 JUIN, 1799.

MISCELLANY.

Snow.—Dr. Rotherham, in his Philosophical Enquiry into the nature and properties of water, says, " one effect of snow, which I can assure my readers of is, that a certain quantity of it, taken up fresh from the ground, and mixed in a flour pudding, will supply the place of eggs, and make it equally light ; the quantity allotted is two table spoonfuls instead of one egg, and if this proportion be much exceeded, the pudding will not adhere together, but will fall to pieces in boiling. I assert this from the experience of my own family, and any one who chuses to try it will find it to be a fact."

Jan. 24. We are assured that the following is an effectual method of extinguishing the burning soot in chimnies : take a little gunpowder, and having humected water for binding it, form it into small masses, and so throw it upon the hearth of the chimney. When it is burnt, and has produced a considerable vapour, a second, and afterwards a third are to be thrown, and so on, as much as is necessary : in a little time the fire is extinguished, and, as it were, choaked by this vapour ; and cakes of inflamed soot are seen to fall from the funnel, till at last not the least vestige of fire appears.

A mechanic at Birmingham has invented a machine for clearing waste lands which, with three horses and six men, will tear up 120 large trees in twelve hours.

VARIETE'S.

La neige.—Le Dr. Rotherham, dans ses recherches Philosophiques dans la nature et la propriété de l'eau, dit " Un des effets de la neige dont je puis assurer mes lecteurs, est, que si vous en prenez une certaine quantité, lorsqu'elle vient de tomber, et la mêlez dans un poudin de fleur, elle suppléera aux œufs et le rendra également léger . la quantité requise est deux cuillères à soupe au lieu d'un œuf, et si on excede cette quantité de beaucoup, le poudin ne se liera point, et tombera par morceau en bouillant. Cet avancé est d'après l'expérience qui en a été faite dans ma propre famille, et quiconque voudra l'essayer, verra que c'est un fait."

Nous sommes assurés que ce qui suit est un moyen efficace d'éteindre la suie qui brule dans les cheminées : prenez un peu de poudre à tirer, et l'ayant humecté avec de l'eau pour lui donner de la consistence, formez-en de petites balles : ensuite jettez-en une sur le foyer de la cheminée, et lorsqu'elle sera brulée, vous en jetterez une seconde, une troisieme, et ainsi tant qu'il sera nécessaire ; elles produiront une vapeur considérable, et en peu de tems le feu s'éteindra de même que s'il étoit étouffé par cette vapeur ; et il tombera par le tuyau de la cheminée des gâteaux de suie enflammée, jusqu'à ce qu'il ne reste plus le moindre vestige de feu.

Un méchanique à Bermingham a inventé une machine pour faire de la terre neuve, qui, au moyen de trois chevaux et six hommes, abattra 120 gros arbres en douze heures.

ity made up mainly of merchants. He was succeeded by another of Wolfe's officers, Guy Carleton later Lord Dorchester, who during two terms as governor was to have a large influence on Canadian history. Carleton after some hesitation decided that Murray's policy of conciliation was the only reasonable one to follow. His views and those of others on both sides of the Atlantic who had come to the same conclusion were embodied in the controversial Quebec Act of 1774. This, in addition to extending the province's boundaries down to the Ohio, restored the old French civil law and granted full rights to Roman Catholics even to the holding of public office. At the same time it rejected demands of the English minority for a representative assembly, an institution to which the French were not accustomed. The Act raised a storm of criticism throughout English-speaking North America and was a factor in bringing about the American Revolution. It is difficult to see, however, what other policy could have been adopted when, as Carleton expressed it in a well-known sentence, it seemed that "barring a catastrophe shocking to think of this country must, to the end of time, be peopled by the [French] Canadian race."

1

3

4

5

12. THE AMERICAN REVOLUTION AND THE LOYALISTS

1. Loyalist encampment at Johnstown on the St. Lawrence, July 6, 1784. By James Peachey
2. Cataraqui (Kingston) with the remains of Fort Frontenac, 1783. By James Peachey
3. Simeon Perkins' house, Liverpool, N.S.
4. The "Loyalist" house, Saint John, N.B., interior
5. The "Loyalist" house, exterior
6. House where the New Brunswick Legislature first met in Fredericton, July, 1788

7. Hay Bay Methodist Church, interior
8. St. Paul's Church, Her Majesty's Chapel of the Mohawks, Brantford

Shortly after the passing of the Quebec Act and partly as a result of it, Carleton's shocking catastrophe did in fact occur: the American Revolutionary War broke out. When it ended in 1783, the only colonies left to Britain in North America were in what is now Canada. Into these there flowed by land and sea over 40,000 Loyalist refugees.

The majority came to Nova Scotia causing it to be divided, New Brunswick and tem-

porarily Cape Breton Island becoming separate provinces in 1784. The population of Nova Scotia had grown slowly since the founding of Halifax in 1749. Some of the earlier arrivals, like Simeon Perkins whose extremely interesting diary has been published, had moved up the coast from New England. Others had come from the British Isles or in the case of Lunenburgers from Western Europe. The arrival of the Loyalists signalled the beginning of much more rapid growth. The newcomers were on the whole men of energy and ability who after initial hardships, quite severe in some cases, were able to re-establish themselves successfully. A number who had

2

6

7

8

been men of wealth and power in the older colonies became so again within the generation — by the time, for example, that the Merritt or "Loyalist" house was built in Saint John in 1810.

Most of the Quebec Loyalists were settled along the St. Lawrence and the north shore of Lake Ontario from the present Quebec boundary westward as far as the Bay of Quinte. By way of preparation, a survey of this region was begun in 1783. One of the surveyors, James Peachey, has left a vivid record in water colour of what he saw.

The Loyalists here were mainly from the farming interior of the older colonies and soon

adjusted to their new environment. Among them were a number of Methodists whose first simple barnlike meeting house was erected at Hay Bay in 1792. The first Anglican church west of the Ottawa had been built in 1785 for a special group of Loyalists, the Six-Nations Indians who had fought under Joseph Brant during the war and been rewarded with "a safe and comfortable retreat" in the Grand River Valley. By 1791, when Quebec was divided into Upper and Lower Canada in order to provide a separate government for the English-speaking western settlements, these latter were already beginning to prosper.

13. EXPLORERS AND FUR TRADERS. I, IN THE NORTH-WEST

1. Beaver Club jewel for Archibald McLellan, 1792, obverse and reverse

2. North West Company canoe's bill of lading, May 6, 1802

3. Montreal, 1812 (detail). By Thomas Davies

4. Hudson's Bay Company canoe

5. Fort William about 1812. By Robert Irvine (real name Crookshank or Cruikshank)

6. Lord Selkirk. From a portrait believed to be by Raeburn

7. York boat

Until the changes initiated by the Loyalist migration began to have their effect in the next generation, the fur trade remained of primary importance to Montreal. By the late eighteenth century, it was concentrated in the north-west, the basins of the Saskatchewan, Mackenzie, and Churchill rivers, where the fur traders such as Alexander Mackenzie were the explorers as well. Because of the large capital requirements of such a far-flung trade, the Montrealers concerned had gradually banded together to form the North West Company with Fort William as a sort of field headquarters to which the furs from the west were brought and exchanged for the trade goods from Montreal. The Nor' Westers of the turn of the century were the aristocrats of the Montreal business world as was symbolized by their exclusive membership in the famous Beaver Club.

Conflict with the Hudson's Bay Company which drew its furs from the same region was inevitable; indeed it was the continuation

3

6

7

4

5

and the climax of the long struggle going back to the seventeenth century between the fur traders of the St. Lawrence and those of the Hudson Bay. Rival posts adjacent to one another sprang up throughout the fur-trading country, but it was at the Red River where the North West Company's line of communications crossed Hudson's Bay territory and where Lord Selkirk planted his settlement that the most serious violence occurred.

Selkirk had had mainly philanthropic motives in acquiring the Red River area from the Hudson's Bay Company and settling it with displaced crofters from the Highlands of Scotland. He and some members of the Company had realized as well, however, the advantages that would result from the settlement becoming a ready source of food for the fur-trading posts. To the Nor'Westers on the other hand, a settlement at that particular location could not but seem a deliberate attempt to block their access to the northwest. They set about therefore to destroy it. The struggle that followed weakened both companies and ruined Selkirk's health and fortune. It ended with the amalgamation of the North West with the Hudson's Bay Company in 1821, a final victory for the

Hudson Bay over the St. Lawrence for fur-trading ascendancy.

After the merger the larger canoes that had long been used by both companies as their principal means of transportation began to be supplemented by the slower but more capacious York boats. These continued to be rowed or sailed vast distances through northern waters until the twentieth century when the outboard motor and the aeroplane brought an end to their usefulness.

V O Y A G E S

MADE IN THE YEARS 1788 AND 1789,

FROM

CHINA TO THE NORTH WEST COAST OF AMERICA.

TO WHICH ARE PREFIXED,

AN INTRODUCTORY NARRATIVE

OF

A VOYAGE performed in 1786, from BENGAL, in the Ship NOOTKA;

OBSERVATIONS ON THE PROBABLE EXISTENCE

OF

A NORTH WEST PASSAGE;

AND SOME ACCOUNT OF

THE TRADE BETWEEN THE NORTH WEST COAST OF AMERICA AND CHINA;
AND THE LATTER COUNTRY AND GREAT BRITAIN.

BY *JOHN MEARES*, ESQ,

LONDON:

PRINTED AT THE Logographic Press;

AND SOLD BY J. WALTER, N° 169, PICCADILLY, OPPOSITE OLD BOND STREET.

M.DCXC.

1 2

In 1793 the North West Company became the first ever to span the continent when one of its partners, Alexander Mackenzie, made his way through the mountains to the Pacific coast. Mackenzie was followed by other Nor'Westers including Simon Fraser and David Thompson, exploring the rivers and mountains, getting to know the relatively advanced natives of the region with their cleverly built weirs and bridges and dugout canoes, and establishing posts for trading with them in furs. By the time of the merger of the North West and the Hudson's Bay Companies in 1821, a valuable trade had been opened up throughout the whole mountainous interior.

Exploration of the coastline by ship was already well under way before Mackenzie's arrival overland. Fifty years before, Bering and Chirikoff on behalf of Russia had sailed along the northern sections. More recently, in the 1770's, Spanish expeditions under Pérez, Heceta, and Quadra had covered the rest. In 1778, Captain Cook of the Royal Navy had voyaged north along the whole coast and through Bering Strait. The summer of Mackenzie's arrival was the middle of three in succession during which Captain George Vancouver, who had been with Cook as a

3

4

5   6

midshipman, was making a thorough survey of every inlet and bay all the way from the Strait of Juan de Fuca to the shores of Alaska.

A very interesting fur trade was also in full swing with the coastal Indians by the time the Nor'Westers put in an appearance. The sea otter with its beautiful rich fur had been discovered by Bering and became known in England with the publication of Cook's *Journals* in 1784. Soon British, Russian, and American ships, heedless of Spanish or other monopolistic claims, were obtaining pelts from the Indians and carrying them across to China where they were in great demand.

Among others engaged in this trade, and no more scrupulous than most, was John Meares, a retired lieutenant of the Royal Navy. Spanish seizure of several of his vessels in Nootka Sound, the headquarters of the sea-otter trade on the west coast of Vancouver Island, resulted in 1790 in a British challenge to Spanish claims in the Pacific. The two countries were brought to the brink of war before Spain was forced by her relative weakness to back down. Meares profited not only from the publication that same year of his *Voyages* but because his highly exaggerated claims for his losses were paid in full.

1

2

3

14. THE WAR OF 1812

1. Brass tomahawk and peace pipe presented to Tecumseh by order of Sir Isaac Brock
2. Sir George Prevost. Cartoon by Robert Dighton
3. Battle of Queenston, Oct. 13, 1812. By Major James B. Dennis, commander of a detachment of the 49th Regiment during the battle
4. Army bill of 1813
5. Sir James Yeo
6. Attack on Fort Oswego, May 6, 1814. By Capt. Steele

American hostility toward Britain, latent since the War of Independence, surged upward in the early nineteenth century as a result both of incidents at sea during Britain's blockade of Napoleonic Europe and of friction in the old Northwest where Britain was suspected of supporting Tecumseh and his discontented Indian followers. It was reinforced by the belief that an attack on Canada, defended only by some 4000 British regulars and a militia of doubtful quality, would easily succeed and would be rewarded by acquisition of at least the western part of Upper Canada where American settlers were already numerous.

What in fact happened after President Madison's declaration of war on June 18, 1812 was that, instead of easy success, three seasons of increasingly vigorous and costly campaigning ended in failure and a negotiated peace that left the boundary unchanged and omitted all mention of American grievances at sea. Failure during the early months was mainly due to American overconfidence and poor leadership combined with a brilliant defensive campaign conducted by the British commander, General Brock. Brock drove back an invasion by a much larger American force which he then followed back across the border

capturing Detroit before turning eastward to the Niagara region where he was similarly successful although at the cost of his own life during the Battle of Queenston. By 1813 the American effort had become more effective but so had British and Canadian resistance, and in 1814 Napoleon's surrender in Europe released thousands of battle-trained British veterans for service in North America.

American strategy throughout the war was distorted by an obsessive preoccupation with the conquest of Upper Canada. Instead of concentrating on the vital Hudson-Champlain-Richelieu warpath to Montreal with the

5

6

objective of cutting Britain's lifeline to the interior, the Americans made their heaviest attacks year after year in the west. Unsatisfactory land communications there made command of the lakes of decisive importance to both sides. An American victory on Lake Erie in 1813 forced a British withdrawal from Detroit during which Tecumseh was killed. On Lake Ontario, a similarly decisive encounter was skilfully avoided for two years by the British commander, Sir James Yeo, and the American, Isaac Chauncey, who instead raided each other's shipping and ports such as York and Oswego.

The war was an unfortunate one for generals, an amazing number of whom on both sides were killed, captured, or court-martialled. Among the latter, except for his death a week before the court was due to convene, would have been Sir George Prevost, the governor-general and commander-in-chief of the British forces in Canada throughout the war. Highly successful earlier as both military commander and civil governor in the West Indies and Nova Scotia, he had been personally responsible for humiliating failures at Sackett's Harbour and in a final major campaign down Lake Champlain.

A by-product of the war was the fact that the issue of army bills in large numbers helped to break down the prejudice that had previously existed—with good cause—against paper money. Although army bills worth five million Spanish dollars were outstanding at the end of the war, all were redeemed in full, paving the way for greater confidence in the use of paper in the future.

1. Covered bridge near St. Martins, N.B.
2. Stage coach in Upper Canada Village, Ontario
3. Corduroy road. Sketch by Titus Hibberts Ware
4. Champlain and St. Lawrence half dollar
5. Montreal and Lachine Railroad Company token
6. The "Samson," first railroad engine in Nova Scotia.

2

1

3

In the generation following the War of 1812 the population of British North America rose very rapidly. Road building became of prime importance both to supplement coastal and inland waterways and to open new areas running back from them and hitherto inaccessible. By 1850 all provinces except Newfoundland had fairly adequate systems of trunk roads. In Newfoundland none existed or would exist for many years outside the immediate vicinity of St. John's.

In Nova Scotia the Halifax-Windsor road and in New Brunswick the Fredericton-Newcastle road were of special importance in that they linked settled areas otherwise cut off from one another except by a long roundabout sea passage. Other main roads circled each of these provinces and met at the Chignecto Isthmus. On Prince Edward Island red clay roads existed but were of less significance because of the many harbours. In Lower Canada the heavily travelled Montreal-Quebec road dated back to the French régime. New roads were extended up the Ottawa and through the Eastern Townships.

In Upper Canada where the most rapid expansion of settlement was taking place road improvement was in greatest demand.

The main trunk from Montreal to Detroit which included Simcoe's old Dundas Street was completed, Yonge Street north from Toronto was improved, the Huron Road was built by the Canada Company through from Galt to Goderich, and the Talbot Roads were built north of Lake Erie and through to Sarnia. As early as the time of its union with Lower Canada in 1841, the province claimed 6000 miles of post roads.

The condition of all British North American roads was best as a rule in winter. It was then, over hard-packed snow and ice, that much of the land transportation of both goods and

4

5

6

passengers took place. Spring virtually closed most roads, and late fall and early winter were almost as bad. Mid-summer was relatively safe, but left exposed all the natural deficiencies of the road surface.

The common surface of early pioneering roads running through heavily wooded British North America was inevitably corduroy. Made by laying logs crossways side by side, the corduroy road is clearly illustrated in the contemporary drawing by Titus H. Ware, for a short time an immigrant lawyer in Orillia. On heavily travelled routes corduroy was being replaced before 1850 by graded

and drained gravel or sometimes by a smooth plank or a hard macadamized surface. Early bridges were often corduroy as well. When plank was used bridges were often covered for protection against the elements. Regular and fairly frequent coach services were provided on the trunk roads of all the provinces and inns were built to care for the relays of horses required and to accommodate travellers.

The use of rails to provide a smooth safe surface for wheeled vehicles went back many generations particularly in the coal mines of Britain. By the 1830's in both England and the United States the steam railway age was

well under way. In British North America the first railroad was the fifteen-mile Champlain and St. Lawrence which opened on July 21, 1836, amid great ceremony, the first two cars being pulled by a small steam engine, the other following drawn by horses. As did many other companies of all sorts in this period, the Champlain and St. Lawrence issued its own currency and seized the opportunity at the same time to advertise its services. In Nova Scotia the "Samson" began in 1839 to draw coal cars the six miles from the Albion Mines to the coast.

1

2

Despite somewhat better roads and the beginning of railways, main reliance throughout this period continued to be placed on water transportation. Improvement of the inland waterways in the vital St. Lawrence-Great Lakes region had begun in the late eighteenth and early nineteenth centuries. Canal building had been undertaken in the St. Lawrence up river from Montreal to permit the passage of flat-bottom batteaux and Durham boats and the North West Company had built a canoe canal on the St. Marys River between Lake Huron and Lake Superior. Transportation

difficulties during the War of 1812 emphasized the need for more and deeper canals. This became still more apparent in the post-war period with the growth of Upper Canadian trade and the rapid introduction of steam boat services following the launching of John Molson's *Accommodation* in 1809. The question took on a new urgency when the state of New York began work on its Erie Canal in 1817. For the St. Lawrence to remain competitive, canals in the regions between Montreal and Lake Ontario and Lake Ontario and Lake Erie became essential.

Work on the Montreal-Lake Ontario route began in the 1820's with the building of the first Lachine Canal, some small canals on the Ottawa River, and the Rideau Canal. The latter, which made use of a chain of lakes and rivers to link the Ottawa River at Bytown (Ottawa) with Lake Ontario 123 miles away, had the great military advantage of providing a transportation route to Upper Canada relatively safe from American attack. Britain, mindful of the St. Lawrence's extreme vulnerability during the War of 1812, agreed to undertake it as a defence project and built it

3

4

5

6 7

Steam-Boat
NOTICE.

The Subscribers announce to the Public, that they have established the following Rates of Freight by their Steam-Boats, between the Ports of Quebec and Montreal, including the intermediate landing places, to commence on the 1st November.

UPWARDS.			DOWNWARDS.		
Pipes,	7s. 6d.	each.	Pipes,	6s. 3d.	each.
Puncheons,	6s. 3d.	do.	Puncheons,	5s.	do.
Hogsheads,	5s.	do.	Hogsheads,	3s. 9d.	do.
Barrels, according to size,	1s. 6d. a 2s	do.	Ashes, p. Barrel,	1s. 8d.	do.
Bales, Cases, &c.	15s. p. ton admeasurement.		Pork, Beef, &c. p. do.	1s. 3d.	do.
			Flour, p. do.	10d.	do.
Iron,	15s. p. ton wt.		Apples, p. do.	7¼d.	do.
Crates, according to size,	6s. 3d. a 7s. 6d. each..		Bales, Cases, &c.	10s. p. ton admeasurement.	
			Butter or Lard in Kegs, not exceeding 60 lbs. weight,	6d.	each.

The Prices for other Articles not enumerated above, to be regulated by the Masters of the Steam-Boats.

JOHN MOLSON & SONS, Agents

St. Lawrence Steam-Boat Company.

Quebec, 31st Oct. 1825.

complete with stone locks and defending blockhouses between 1826 and 1832. The cost finally amounted to about £1,000,000 making it the most expensive military work built up to that time anywhere in North America.

The problem of a waterway between Lake Ontario and Lake Erie that would bypass Niagara Falls was tackled vigorously by a St. Catharines businessman William Hamilton Merritt. Organizing a private company, he began work in 1824 and after overcoming tremendous financial and physical difficulties watched the first ships pass through in 1829. The canal was not really in satisfactory shape however and would not be for many years. Poor wooden locks and an uncertain · water supply meant that much work still had to be done and much more money spent, a considerable part of it being obtained from the provincial government which finally assumed control in 1841.

By that time, when the union of Upper and Lower Canada had taken place, the round-about Rideau and the unsatisfactory Welland were still all that the new province had to show for the great efforts of the 1820's. Agreement was general that a complete system of St. Lawrence canals nine feet deep had become necessary together with a corresponding deepening and improvement of the Welland. Fortunately money had become available through Britain's willingness to guarantee a £1,500,000 loan as a means of persuading Upper Canada to join the Union. The 1840's as a result became Canada's great canal building period and before their conclusion the desired waterway was completed.

1. Emigrants on board the *Cambridge*, July 19, 1844. By T. H. Ware
2. Log house near Orillia, Upper Canada. By T. H. Ware
3. Col. Thomas Talbot
4. John Galt
5. Canada Company Office, Toronto, in 1834. By J. G. Howard

1

The 25 years up to 1851 were years of rapidly expanding settlement in Upper Canada, or Canada West as it came to be known after its union with Lower Canada in 1841. In 1825 the population had been approximately 158,000, about one-third that of Lower Canada. By 1851 it had jumped to 952,000 and for the first time it exceeded that of the older partner. The transformation that had taken place was mainly the result of an influx of immigrants from the United Kingdom.

Many of these had come as individuals or as family units. Those with sufficient capital bought land that had already been cleared by what were virtually professional pioneers. Others had to buy uncleared lands themselves and begin cutting and burning the trees trying to eke out a sparse living for some years among the stumps. Still others, without any resource but their strong backs, obtained work, possibly on some canal building project, until their savings had become sufficient for them to make a start on the road to independence.

In addition to individual initiatives of this sort, a number of private and public efforts were made to assist and encourage immigration. The two most important were those of Colonel Thomas Talbot and the Canada Company.

Talbot, a member of a socially prominent Anglo-Irish family, had first come to Canada as a young aide-de-camp to Lieutenant-Governor Simcoe. He had returned in 1803 to begin his colonizing activities in the region north of Lake Erie. A figure of controversy in his own day and since, Talbot was nevertheless extremely successful in opening up a large area by means of excellent roads and getting it cleared and occupied by industrious settlers; those lacking in industry he ruthlessly ejected.

The Canada Company was the creation

2

3

4

5

of another unusual and energetic man—John Galt, a well-known Scottish novelist. Galt possessed great imagination and a highly contagious variety of enthusiasm. With these assets, he was responsible for bringing together a group of London investors, for conducting extensive negotiations with the British government, and for obtaining the latter's agreement to sell to the company, chartered in June 1825, over two million acres in Upper Canada made up of the Huron Tract and the Crown Reserves. Galt arrived in Canada in 1826 to direct the undertaking but was soon in difficulty with both the provincial government

and the company in London and had to be replaced. His, however, had been an essential contribution to the largest colonization attempt in Upper Canada.

Pioneer farming, especially on land that was only partially cleared, and life in a log cabin isolated in the bush called for courage and endurance on the part of both men and women. The first cash crop was produced as the trees were burned—potash made by leaching and boiling the ashes. In 1831 when clearing was at its height, some 8500 tons of potash made by burning more than 4,000,000 tons of hardwood were exported. Canada

was at that time (as she has become again thanks to the Saskatchewan deposits) a leading world producer of potash and supplied three-quarters of Britain's requirements for her textile and glass industries. When clearing was completed, wheat became the major crop for sale. By the 1840's, its cultivation had been made easier by the introduction, mainly from the United States, of improved agricultural implements—cast iron ploughs, seed drills, lighter harrows, and even primitive threshing machines.

18. LUMBERING AND SHIPBUILDING IN THE MARITIMES

1. Shipbuilding near Dorchester, N.B.
2. Lumberers on the St. John River. By James Cumming Clarke
3. Steam lumber mill at Millidgeville, N.B., By E. J. Russell
4. Clearing the town plot at Stanley, N.B., 1834. By W. P. Kay

The Atlantic region was on the whole only slightly less prosperous and optimistic than Upper Canada in the 25-year period leading up to mid-century. Its total population rose by about 160 per cent and its fish, timber, and ships were in wide demand. Its seafarers were well known throughout the oceans of the world.

Except on Prince Edward Island, and in a few rich valleys of Nova Scotia and New Brunswick, there was little agriculture. In contrast to Upper and Lower Canada, the Atlantic region was an over-all importer rather than exporter of foodstuffs. The only major attempt at the sort of colonization undertaken by the Canada Company was that of the Nova Scotia and New Brunswick Land Company to settle a 500,000-acre tract in central New Brunswick. Clearing began in 1834 at Stanley and other preparations were made for the reception of settlers. Lithographed drawings by artists such as W. P. Kay were given wide circulation as part of a vigorous publicity campaign. The end result, however, was complete failure.

Several explanations for this have been suggested, but the fundamental fact was that the forests of New Brunswick were more attractive than most of its fields. Burning the trees in order to make way for agriculture was the only thing to do in land-locked Upper Canada. In New Brunswick the logs could be floated down river to a mill, and the lumber or square timber either shipped off to markets of Britain or used in an adjacent shipyard. The timber trade had the disadvantage of undergoing violent ups and downs. Moralists complained of the rowdy improvident life lived in the woods and the way in which its

3

4

attractions interfered with more stable agricultural development. These complaints were justified. More persuasive, however, was the knowledge that fortunes could be made (as well as lost) by lumbering and shipbuilding and that few indeed could be made by farming in New Brunswick.

Nova Scotia depended far less on lumbering than did New Brunswick, but the two were much on a par in shipbuilding and shipping. Nova Scotia built larger numbers of ships but more of them were small fishing and coastal vessels and New Brunswick's total

tonnage was usually greater. Certain ports acquired special reputation as major shipbuilding centres. St. Andrews and Saint John in New Brunswick and Pictou, Yarmouth, Liverpool, and Lunenburg in Nova Scotia were perhaps best known. In both provinces, however, right up until the end of the wooden-ship era building continued all along the coasts and sometimes far upstream.

Coal and gypsum mining and a much larger fishing industry gave Nova Scotia's economy generally a diversity not shared by that of New Brunswick—or indeed by

those of Newfoundland and Prince Edward Island. Newfoundland continued to depend almost entirely on her cod fisheries. Prince Edward Island had some fishing, but her rich red soil was already making her better known as the "garden of the gulf."

1

2

3

7

19. FAMILY COMPACT SOCIETY

1. "Clifton," Judge T. C. Haliburton's house, Nova Scotia. Completed 1836

2. Interior of "Clifton"

3. "Mount Uniacke," Attorney General R. J. Uniacke's house, Nova Scotia. Completed 1815

4. E. B. Chandler's house, Dorchester, New Brunswick. Completed 1840

5. "Dundurn," Sir Allan MacNab's house, Hamilton, Upper Canada. Completed 1835.

6. Sir Allan MacNab

7. Christ Church Cathedral, Fredericton, N.B. Completed 1853

8. St. Andrew's Presbyterian Church, Niagara-on-the-Lake, Upper Canada. Completed 1831

Log cabins and timber shanties were not characteristic of the whole of society in the period following the War of 1812. From the first arrival of the Loyalists, conscious efforts had been made to create a class structure in British North America similar to that of the mother country and clearly different from that of the democratic and republican United States. War and post-war anti-Americanism assisted this policy and something like "family compacts" became entrenched as privileged governing classes in all of the provinces.

Nowhere was this more the case than in the Maritimes. R. J. Uniacke and T. C. Hali-burton in Nova Scotia and E. B. Chandler in New Brunswick are good examples of the class there despite, or perhaps because of, the fact that none was typical. Uniacke had arrived to Nova Scotia from Ireland *via* the West Indies in 1774. From 1797 until his death over thirty years later, he was the province's Attorney General and the holder of various other lucrative offices. T. C. Haliburton, son of a pre-Loyalist father and a Loyalist mother, succeeded his father in a judgeship—and wrote *Sam Slick* and *The Clockmaker*. E. B. Chandler was the grandson of a prominent Loyalist and an able and well-known lawyer and office holder, and eventually lieutenant-governor of New Brunswick. Men of strikingly different personality and different generations, they nevertheless showed the most common "family compact" characteristics—Loyalist or pre-Loyalist background, membership in the dominant Church of England, legal training, and long profitable careers in government office. The houses they built and lavishly furnished show how far the standard of living of this class had advanced beyond the backwoods.

In Upper Canada where the term "family compact" originated, it was applied parti-

5

8

6

cularly to the group centring around the Reverend John Strachan and John Beverley Robinson. Exemplifying the same viewpoint in its last stage was Sir Allan MacNab. The son of one of Simcoe's aides-de-camp, MacNab was a hero of the War of 1812 at the age of fifteen and displayed similar dash and resolution during the rebellion of 1837. By that time he had already built up the largest law practice in Hamilton, had completed "Dundurn," and had been elected to the provincial assembly of which he would remain a member through nine successive parliaments. His extensive business interests included the presidency of the Great Western Railway. From 1854 to 1856 he was premier of the United Province of Canada. His replacement by the more moderate conservative, John A. Macdonald, marked the disappearance of "family compact" ideals from Canadian politics.

In a society in which some had become affluent and where religion played a major role, churches were among the important building projects of almost every community. Size, design and material varied depending upon the wealth of the congregation, denominational symbolism, and current taste. St. Andrew's, Niagara-on-the-Lake, is an excellent and comparatively rare example of the Greek revival style so popular in the United States. Its republican symbolism made this style suspect in the anti-American atmosphere of Canada. Christ Church, Fredericton, on the other hand, as befitted an Anglican foundation, was clearly, indeed assertively, part of the Anglo-Catholic Gothic revival that was sweeping England in the 1840's and '50's.

1

20. CONTROVERSY OVER EDUCATION

1. McGill College, 1860
2. Seminary of Nicolet. Built 1832
3. John Strachan
4. Egerton Ryerson
5. Upper Canada College in 1835. By Thomas Young
6. University College, University of Toronto, during construction (1856-59)

2

British North America's growing population and advancing standard of living encouraged a demand in the 1820's and '30's for improved educational facilities at a more advanced level. Some initial responses were made, but substantial achievement was delayed for several decades by bitter controversy—controversy that formed part of the wider conflict going on between the old social order and its opponents and included questions of responsible government and a whole range of other reforms.

On the side of the old order were those who like the Reverend John Strachan believed in the preservation of the British connection and the staving off of American democratic and republican ideas by duplicating as far as possible the British social system. They assumed that the British tradition of state support for Anglican-controlled schools and colleges would be followed and that the primary role of these would be to educate children of the privileged classes. Equality for all became the opposing demand of "reformers" like the Methodist, Egerton Ryerson. Many came to believe that this could best be achieved by establishing non-denominational state-supported institutions of the sort becoming common in the United States.

King's College, York (Toronto), with Strachan as president, and a grammar school, Upper Canada College, both to receive state support but to be under Anglican control, became focal points of the dispute in Upper Canada. Upper Canada College was brought into being successfully but with the coming of responsible government, the legislature passed an act in 1850 transforming King's into the "godless" University of Toronto. Strachan went on stubbornly to found Trinity as its successor. Meanwhile the Methodists had founded Victoria at Cobourg with

3

4

5

6

Ryerson as first president and the Presbyterians Queen's at Kingston. The Roman Catholics soon added St. Michael's at Toronto. University College, a non-denominational college of the University of Toronto, was completed in 1859.

The pattern in the rest of English-speaking British North America was much the same with two exceptions: in Prince Edward Island no advance was made beyond the secondary level and in Newfoundland none beyond the primary; and in Nova Scotia, Dalhousie, and in Lower Canada, McGill, originated as non-denominational institutions.

Presbyterian influence was strong however at Dalhousie and Anglican at McGill and neither achieved stability until the 1850's or 1860's when the climate of opinion had become more favourable to secular education.

French-speaking Lower Canada had, of course, its own educational traditions about which there was no controversy at that time. In 1852 the old Seminary of Quebec received a royal charter for the creation of Laval University along the lines of a French university with several professional faculties and a faculty of arts. The teaching in the latter would be done in affiliated classical colleges of

which there were nine scattered throughout the province, in addition to the old seminaries at Quebec and Montreal. Typical was the Seminary at Nicolet in a building completed in 1832, a fine example of French classicism designed by Jerome Demers, director of the Seminary of Quebec, in collaboration with Thomas Baillairgé, the most outstanding of the famous family of sculptors and architects.

21. THE REBELLIONS AND RESPONSIBLE GOVERNMENT

1. "Back view of Church at St. Eustache and Dispersion of the Insurgents, Dec. 14, 1837." By Capt. Lord Charles Beauclerk, Royal Regiment

2. James B. Tyrrell, one of the rebels banished to Van Dieman's Land.

3. Louis-Joseph Papineau

4. William Lyon Mackenzie

5. Sir Francis Bond Head

6. Earl of Durham

7. Earl of Elgin

8. Robert Baldwin

9. Louis-Hippolyte LaFontaine

10. Extracts from the Montreal *Gazette*

As dissension grew during the 1830's between the ruling classes in Upper and Lower Canada and their opponents, threats of violence began to be made. Moderate reformers like Louis-Hippolyte LaFontaine and Robert Baldwin drew back in dismay. Others pressed on led by Louis-Joseph Papineau and William Lyon Mackenzie, men of fierce, reckless determination as is clearly displayed even in the photographs taken of them in later life. Fighting began and was most bitter in Lower Canada. The bloodiest engagement took place on December 14, 1837, at St. Eustache where, on the approach of some 2000 soldiers led by the commander-in-chief Sir John Colborne himself, the rebels barricaded themselves in the church. Driven out when the adjacent convent and presbytery were set on fire, some seventy were slain and most of the rest taken prisoners.

In Upper Canada, the enthusiastic support

4

5

6

7

8

9

The Gazette.

MONTREAL,
Tuesday Evening, May 29.

Every one of Her Majesty's loyal subjects in British America will rejoice to learn, that the troops under the immediate command of Lieutenant Colonel Wetherall, have succeeded in dislodging the leaders of the Lower Canadian rebels, and their deluded followers, from the first position they ventured to assume at the village of St. Charles, on the *Richelieu* River; the particulars of which will be found in another place. This may be denominated as not a less fortunate than triumphant blow which has been given to the hydra-headed monster, that has dared to exhibit itself in this land of peace and unquestionable liberty. But we must warn our readers, that the victory is still far from being complete. There are yet more traitors in the Province than those, who are most favourably disposed to think well of the inhabitants of French origin, would reck of; and, should the issue of events prove different from what they have done, this city and the neighbourhood would bear ample testimony to the truth of the assertion. We avow it, there is every reason to believe, that Montreal is full of clandestine arms; and that there are many treasonable and disaffected individuals prepared to wield them, the moment that a favourable opportunity presents itself. If the case were otherwise, why

The *Toronto Colonist*, of the 12th instant, contains a postscript, stating that at eight o'clock that morning, Samuel Lount and Peter Mathews had been executed for High Treason, in conformity to the sentence of the law passed against them. They walked with a firm step to the scaffold; and were assisted in their devotions by the Rev. Mr. Richardson. An immense concourse of spectators had assembled to witness the execution; but the greatest order was preserved during the whole of this melancholy scene.

Tuesday Evening, May 29.

Arrival of the Earl of Durham.

We have received private letters this morning from Quebec, from which we learn, that Her Majesty's ship *Hastings*, having His Excellency the Earl of Durham, family and suite on board, had arrived on Sunday, at one o'clock in the afternoon. It was reported that His Lordship was to disembark yesterday at two o'clock, and assume the Administration of the Government of the Province.

10

given the old order by the lieutenant-governor, Sir Francis Bond Head, and his recklessness in sending all the regular troops off to Lower Canada in November, as soon as trouble there began, provoked Mackenzie and his followers to try to seize power in Toronto. Their invasion down Yonge Street early in December was a complete fiasco. Mackenzie managed to escape to the United States but two of his chief lieutenants, Samuel Lount and Peter Mathews, were captured and executed.

Order was eventually restored without too much difficulty despite some quite substantial attacks across the border by rebels and their American sympathizers. The major problem, that of finding a permanent remedy for Canada's troubles, was entrusted to the most important British statesman ever to administer British North American affairs, Lord Durham. Durham spent only four months in 1838 in Canada before returning to present his famous *Report* to the British government. In it, he recommended the reunion of Upper and Lower Canada and the granting of responsible government. The first of these recommendations was duly implemented by the Act of Union of 1840. The second seemed altogether too radical — incompatible with continued unity of the Empire. It was not until well on in the 1840's when Durham's son-in-law, Lord Elgin, became governor general that a change took place. Under his wise leadership the new system was successfully introduced, Baldwin and Lafontaine forming the first truly responsible government in 1848.

1

2 3

22. THE OPENING OF THE GRAND TRUNK
RAILWAY

1. Notman stereoscopic view of Victoria
Bridge under construction
2. Beginning the Victoria Bridge
3. Announcement of opening of Grand
Trunk to Toronto
4. Sleeping car interior
5. Sleeping car interior
6. Early wood-burning locomotive

With their constitutional problems solved for the time being at least, Canadians, politicians and all, turned their attention enthusiastically to railways, making the 1850's the first of Canada's great railway ages. In 1850 there were only 66 miles of track in the whole of British North America. By 1860, 2000 more had been laid and the Grand Trunk, stretching from Sarnia to Rivière du Loup and Portland, Maine, had become the world's longest railway under single management. What had happened was that Canadians, and Maritimers as well, had suddenly become conscious of the fact that their splendid inland waterways, even after the laborious canal building of recent decades, were being rendered inadequate by the extensive railway building going on south of the border. Ports like Montreal, Halifax, and Saint John and even inland centres like Sherbrooke and Guelph had come to realize that their futures depended on railway connections with the rest of the continent. And individuals saw in these great new undertakings opportunities unequalled even in the days of the fur trade to make fortunes for themselves.

4

5

6

Canada's first major railway was the St. Lawrence and Atlantic between Montreal and Portland, Maine. While it was being pushed to completion in the early 1850's, under the able leadership of A. T. Galt, Sir Allan MacNab's Great Western was being built between Buffalo and Detroit, with a line out to Hamilton and Toronto. The obvious desirability of linking these systems was behind the original conception of the Grand Trunk. As it turned out, the Great Western remained independent (until a much later date) and the Grand Trunk was extended to Sarnia instead. The St. Lawrence and Atlantic and Grand Trunk did come together, however, their physical connection being the great tubular Victoria Bridge, the first across the St. Lawrence and one of the engineering wonders of the day—a favourite subject of Montreal's best-known early photographer, William Notman, and of those interested in his popular stereoscopic views.

The announcement of the opening of the Grand Trunk service between Montreal and Toronto in 1856 draws attention to inconvenient time differences that then existed between Canadian cities and the railway's decision to ignore them. It was no accident that in due course it would be a man closely connected with the building of Canada's long east-west lines of railways, Sandford Fleming, who would take the initiative in getting the Canadian and American railways, and eventually in 1884 the whole world, to adopt standard time.

2

1

23. AN EXPANDING ECONOMY

1. Suspension Bridge at Niagara. Built 1851-55
2. *Great Eastern* at Heart's Content, Newfoundland, 1866
3. Sir Francis Hincks
4. Bank of Upper Canada, Hamilton, Canada West, *c.* 1860
5. The Three-Penny Beaver. First proof
6. Bank of Upper Canada penny, 1854, obverse and reverse
7. City Hall, Woodstock, Ont.
8. Goderich street corner, probably 1866

In a bustling railway-building age towns soon became cities and began to lay down wide plank sidewalks and build proud new city halls. Major construction undertakings such as the wire-cable suspension bridge at Niagara, the first of its kind, were entered upon without hesitation and a general air air of optimism prevailed.

Simultaneously with railway-building two other improvements in communications took place, the introduction of prepaid and much reduced postal fees and the rapid extension of telegraph and cable lines. The first of these, the postal revolution inaugurated by Rowland

Hill in Britain in the 1840's, was brought to Canada with the introduction of the "Three-Penny Beaver" designed by the ubiquitous Sandford Fleming in 1851. New Brunswick and Nova Scotia began using stamps that same year and the other colonies followed shortly. It was in 1851 as well that Hugh Allan became President of the Montreal Telegraph Company and began a remarkable 20-year extension of its lines from about 500 miles to 20,000, making them the longest in Canada. The first Atlantic cable was successfully laid in 1858 but it failed after a few weeks. Permanent trans-Atlantic operations began

only after the cable ship *Great Eastern* reached Heart's Content, Newfoundland, on July 27, 1866, with a line that it had begun reeling out at Ventura, Ireland, two weeks before.

Along with improved communications British North America's expanding economy required enlarged banking facilities. The first permanent bank in Canada was the Bank of Montreal organized in 1817, but it was followed shortly by others and by 1867 there were 28 banks with a total of 123 branches in the new Dominion. One of the most important had been the Bank of Upper Canada chartered in 1821. It was the government

3

4

5

6

7

8

bank of that province and closely associated with the Family Compact party. It began to lose ground after union with Lower Canada and the coming of responsible government and in 1863 it was displaced in its special connection with the government by the Bank of Montreal. In 1866 it closed its doors, the first major bank failure in Canadian history.

A function of pre-Confederation banks had been to issue notes. Thanks to the success of the War-of-1812 army notes, these met with considerable acceptance as paper money, but they had the disadvantage of being redeemable only at a heavy discount. The banks, along with other commercial enterprises, also issued tokens in smaller amounts to make up for deficiencies in the coinage. Francis Hincks whose influence in financial matters was paramount in the 1840's and early '50's made every effort to get a uniform currency accepted throughout British North America based on the American decimal system. Decimal systems were finally introduced in Canada and New Brunswick and to a degree in Nova Scotia between 1858 and 1860 but did not become completely uniform until after Confederation.

1

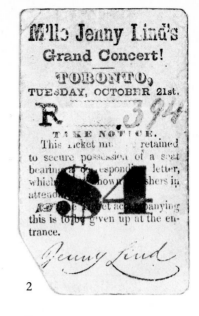

2

3

By the 1850's, life in the several provincial capitals was beginning to take on some degree of colour and sophistication. This was not quite true perhaps of Charlottetown which remained an overgrown country village of less than 7000 inhabitants, or of St. John's, Newfoundland, still recovering from the disastrous fire of 1846. Fredericton was small and remote, but the quiet beauty of its setting on the banks of the St. John, its new cathedral, and its lingering tradition of a Loyalist élite gave it a special character of its own. Halifax was a major defence centre as was Quebec. Their streets, lined with heavy stone buildings, and their massive citadels gave both an air of age and stability belied somewhat by the bustling cosmopolitan nature of their populations.

Of them all, Toronto was undergoing the most rapid change. Capital of Upper Canada until 1841 and then in the 1850's alternating with Quebec as capital of the United Province, Toronto had become far different from the sleepy York of 1831 when its parliament buildings were new. Improvements in water and land transportation, including the opening of the Grand Trunk Railway to Montreal in 1856, had made it the metropolitan centre for the whole booming western part of the province.

Its enhanced stature was reflected in the changes taking place in its newspapers. The most powerful of these, George Brown's *Globe,* moved into new quarters at 22 King Street West in 1853 and acquired a new rapid-action rotary press run by a larger steam engine. With these facilities it expanded from thrice-weekly to daily publication. Three other newspapers out of the total of 14 published in the city had also become dailies by that time.

Perhaps the most obvious mark of Toronto's

4

5

7

6

progress was its new Crystal Palace opened for the 1858 Exhibition. Ever since London's Great Exhibition and wonder-inspiring Crystal Palace of 1851, these large cast-iron and glass structures had become the major status symbols of cities throughout the British Empire and the United States. Toronto's, built two years before Montreal's, was designed by Sandford Fleming and Collingwood Schreiber who in later life would be successively chief engineers of the Canadian Pacific Railway.

Another building which had recently added to Toronto's prestige, was St. Lawrence Hall with its 1,000-seat auditorium and other facilities for concerts, lectures, fashionable balls, and public meetings of all sorts. A major event of its first year, 1851, had been the concert by Jenny Lind, the famous "Swedish nightingale" who was touring the United States and Canada under the management of that great showman and temperance lecturer, P. T. Barnum.

The visit of the Prince of Wales to Canada in 1860 gave Toronto an opportunity, along with other towns and cities, to put on a festive appearance, erect welcoming arches across its thoroughfares, and indulge in a gay round of receptions and balls. From Toronto, the Prince took one of the favourite excursions of the day, a trip to Niagara Falls, not only to see that great natural spectacle, but also to watch Blondin cross the gorge on his tightrope. A young midshipman of the Prince's party reporting the second part of Blondin's act, which was to cross with a man on his back, observed: "he looked alright, but the man was very pale."

1

2

3

25. ARCTIC EXPLORERS: SIR JOHN FRANKLIN
AND OTHERS

1. Fort Franklin near west end of Great
   Bear Lake, winter of 1825-26. By George
   Back

2. Franklin expedition on the Yellowknife,
   May 30, 1820. By Robert Hood

3. Franklin expedition on ice of Point
   Lake, near Coppermine River, June 25,
   1821. By George Back

4. Sir John Franklin

5. Sir John Rae

6. Hudson's Bay Company Chief Factor
   J. L. Cotter

7. Hudson's Bay Company five shilling note

8. Making a kayak, 1870. Photographed by
   J. L. Cotter

9. Remains of Franklin expedition discovered in 1931

Following the Napoleonic Wars the British
Admiralty resumed the scientific explorations that it had been undertaking throughout
the world in the late eighteenth century. For
the next forty years it took a special interest

in the Canadian Arctic and accomplished
much through the efforts of Ross, Franklin,
Parry, Beechey, Rae, and many others.
The most intensive explorations took place
in the decade after 1847 when the search
began for Franklin, lost with his whole
third expedition. Some fifty search parties
were organized, private and public, and much
new information about the Arctic was incidentally accumulated. In 1853 Rae discovered
Franklin relics in Eskimo possession. With
this clue to guide him, M'Clintock in 1857
finally reached the site off King William
Island where the expedition had spent its

last two years jammed in the ice and recovered a document telling of Franklin's death. As late as 1931 skeletons of other members of Franklin's party were found by a Hudson's Bay Company factor.

Much of the information acquired during these years was made known in accounts published by the explorers themselves. Care was taken to add to their usefulness by providing accurate illustrations. Franklin, for example, selected the midshipmen for his first expedition, George Back and Robert Hood, largely for their artistic ability. Hood, weakened by the hardships of what turned out to be an almost disastrous expedition, was murdered toward its end by a crazed Indian guide. Back proved himself one of the hardiest of Arctic travellers and was with Franklin again on his second journey recording the relatively comfortable winter headquarters, Fort Franklin, that experience had shown to be necessary. By the end of the period, photography was taking the place of water colour. J. L. Cotter, a Hudson's Bay Company factor at Moose River in the 1860's, was one of the earliest photographers of Arctic scenes.

The Hudson's Bay Company, as the organization on which the area's economy was coming largely to depend, had played a significant role throughout these explorations. In addition to the important journeys of its own servants, Rae, Dease, and Thomas Simpson, its network of posts and its knowledge of the Indians and Eskimo made its support invaluable particularly to land expeditions such as Franklin's first two.

1

2

26. PRAIRIE EXPLORERS: HIND AND PALLISER

1. White Mud Portage, Winnipeg River. By Paul Kane

2. Cree Indian Buffalo Pound. By George Back, February, 1820

3. "Indian hunter pursuing the Buffalo early in the spring when the snow is sufficiently frozen to bear men but the animal breaks through and cannot run." By Peter Rindisbacker

4. Hind expedition, encampment on the Red River. By H. L. Hime

5. John Palliser and James Hector

The western interior had become known to the La Vérendrye's, Anthony Henday, and others in the eighteenth century. It was known in part, of course, to Red River settlers like Peter Rindisbacker and Hudson's Bay traders such as those with whom Paul Kane travelled for two years in the 1840's. Franklin had passed through a section in 1820 on his way to the Coppermine River and had paused to observe a Cree buffalo pound with a tree in the centre: "they occasionally place a man in the tree to sing to the presiding spirit as the buffalos are advancing," he wrote in explanation of Back's sketch.

But Franklin's interest in the west was only incidental and that of the Hudson's Bay Company was limited to the fur trade. No scientific study of the west comparable to that begun by Franklin in the north was undertaken until the 1850's. Then, faced with growing demands that the Hudson's Bay Company be dispossessed and the region opened to settlement and with vigorous controversy as to whether it was suitable for this purpose or not, the British and Canadian governments both sent out expeditions almost simultaneously to make detailed investigations.

Captain Palliser's British expedition arrived

5

3

at Fort William to begin its work in June 1857, six weeks before the Canadians. With it as geologist was Dr. James Hector, according to Palliser "the most accurate mapper of original country I have seen." For three years Palliser and Hector surveyed the whole region as far as the Rockies and then passed through these to the coast returning to England by sea. The Canadian expedition under H. Y. Hind, professor of chemistry and geology at Trinity College, Toronto, and S. J. Dawson, a civil engineer, spent two years making a very detailed examination of the country as far west as the present Alberta-Saskatchewan border. With it was H. L. Hime, the first photographer west of the Great Lakes.

Although they differed in scope and to some extent in conclusion, the reports of the two expeditions combined to establish the outlines of prairie geography much as we understand them today. Hind was more optimistic as to the area fit for settlements. Palliser placed greater emphasis on the arid southern triangle that has been given his name. In general, both were in agreement that large stretches of fertile land existed entirely suitable for settlement.

1

2

5

7

27. THE RED RIVER SETTLEMENT

1. Sir George Simpson
2. Bishop A. A. Taché
3. Kildonan Presbyterian Church. By H. L. Hime
4. St. Andrew's Anglican Church. By H. L. Hime
5. Upper Fort Garry. By H. L. Hime
6. St. Boniface Cathedral and convent. By H. L. Hime
7. Lower Fort Garry
8. Red River ox cart

By 1857 when it was visited by Palliser and Hind and photographed by Hime, the Red River settlement was no longer the small isolated colony struggling against extinction that it had been in the time of Selkirk. Its population was still not large—probably about six or seven thousand—but the Scottish agricultural community uneasily set down in the midst of a fur-trading world had been transformed into a bustling Hudson's Bay Company supply and communications centre inhabited mainly by half-breeds, the majority of them French-speaking.

The livelihood of the half-breeds depended very largely on the fur trade. Some manned the York boats that plied the waterways between Hudson Bay and the settlement and up the Saskatchewan and into the far north-west. Others drove long lines of Red River carts up and down the trail from St. Paul which was rapidly becoming in the 1850's the leading supply and export route of the settlement; 300 carts are estimated to have used it in 1857. More numerous still were the buffalo hunters who provided the staple food of the fur trade, pemmican. The annual spring buffalo hunts were highly organized large-scale expeditions out into the prairies in which as early as 1840 over a thousand carts took part.

3

4

6

8

Landmarks in the colony itself were its two forts and its churches. Fort Garry had been built as a major Hudson's Bay Company post immediately after the 1821 union with the North West Company. Located at the junction of the Red and the Assiniboine Rivers it had been severely damaged in the great flood of 1826. The newly appointed governor-in-chief, George Simpson—who would hold that office until his death in 1860—thought it preferable to rebuild 19 miles downstream on a safer site and one that was below the difficult St. Andrews Rapids. Hardly had Lower Fort Garry been completed there in 1833, however, when he changed his mind and decided that the Company's headquarters in the colony should, after all, remain on the original site. Upper Fort Garry was accordingly completed in 1835. Across the river, in St. Boniface, a fine Roman Catholic cathedral was built by Bishop Provencher only to be destroyed by fire in 1860 in the time of his successor, the famous Bishop Taché. The Anglicans built several smaller churches and the substantial St. Andrew's before the Presbyterians finally, in 1854, completed through their own efforts the church at Kildonan originally promised them by Lord Selkirk.

1

2

3

4

5

6

28. BRITISH COLUMBIA.

I, THE FRASER–CARIBOO GOLD RUSHES

1. Kwakiutl totem poles at Alert Bay, 1924
2. Grave pole near old Bella Coola Indian village
3. Sir James Douglas
4. S. S. *Beaver*
5. The steamer *Onward* on the Fraser
6. Sir Matthew Begbie
7. Stage coach
8. Ox team at the Clinton Hotel
9. Mule train on the Cariboo Road

Between 1821 when the North West and Hudson's Bay Companies were united and 1858 when the first gold rush to the Fraser made the introduction of crown colony government necessary in British Columbia, the Hudson's Bay Company was the responsible British authority west as well as east of the Rockies. Significant changes took place during this period. The fur trade was reorganized and brigade trails through the interior improved. Sufficient progress was made in agriculture to enable the supply not only of the Hudson's Bay posts but of the Russian as well. The first lumber and flour mills were built and in 1852 the Nanaimo

coal mines were opened.

A particularly imaginative and successful experiment was the sailing from England around Cape Horn of the *Beaver* and her fitting out with engines and paddles to make her in 1836 the first steamship in the Pacific. The *Beaver* gave good service to the Company and later owners for many years before going aground off Vancouver in 1888.

One of a number of effects all of this had on the Indians was that it enabled them to develop beyond previous possibilities their traditional wood-carving skills. With European tools and lavish amounts of ship's paint they created a flourishing totem-pole art for

9

which they remained known well into the twentieth century.

The gold rush to the Fraser in 1858 and then on to the Cariboo after the William's Creek discoveries in 1861 was one of the spectacular events of Canadian history. During the first season, at least 25,000 men arrived mainly from California and the influx continued year after year. By 1863 some 4000 men were working the gravel along seven miles of William's Creek alone, 400 miles beyond the head of navigation on the Fraser, and the rest of the Cariboo had been occupied as well. On the coast Victoria had been transformed from a quiet village

into a bustling outpost of San Francisco. Presiding over it all with the assurance gained from forty years in the fur trade going back to the days of the North West Company was James Douglas, long the senior Hudson's Bay Company official west of the mountains and, after 1858, governor of the new crown colony of British Columbia. Assisting him was Judge Matthew Begbie, one of the main reasons for the comparative absence of lawlessness in the Cariboo, and a force of 165 Royal Engineers who not only helped maintain order but blasted out of the mountain sides some of the most difficult sections of the famous Cariboo Road.

1

2

3

4

28. BRITISH COLUMBIA AND THE GOLD RUSHES:
II, IN THE CARIBOO

1. Billy Phinney washing tailings with a hand rocker on Old Caledonia. F. Dally photograph, 1868
2. A Cariboo wheel- or trundle-barrow
3. Wheel and flume on the Davis claim. F. Dally photograph, 1868
4. The last of the Cariboo camels
5. The Cameron claim. "Cariboo Cameron" seated with mining pan on knee. C. Fulton photograph, Aug. 20, 1863

Transportation problems were the most serious faced by the miners of the Cariboo. Steamers could make their way up the Fraser as far as Hope and eventually Yale but beyond were still some 400 miles of difficult trail or waterway to Barkerville in the heart of the Cariboo. Men struggled through in the early days with packs on their backs or on the backs of horses and mules. Some used ingenious centre-wheeled barrows. Frank Laumeister bought U.S. Army surplus camels but had to abandon them after two years when their smell and their biting and kicking brought too many lawsuits from other packers. The solution decided on by Governor Douglas, the building of an 18-foot wide Cariboo Road, was a daring one but it was successfully completed between 1862 and 1865 by the Royal Engineers and private contractors. Up and down it as it was being built there gradually came into operation the famous BX or Barnard's Express Stage Coach Line, soon to have one of the longest runs in North America, and plodding ox and mule trains began to put in an appearance hauling supplies of all sorts.

In the mining region itself, towns rapidly sprang up, hillsides being denuded of their trees to provide the timber for shacks and mine workings. The latter were sometimes

5

quite extensive because, while the first gold could be panned from the stream bed where it had recently been deposited by the rushing water, far greater quantities were to be found up to 20 or 30 feet beneath the surface covered by the silt and debris of thousands of centuries. To get at this shafts had to be sunk, tunnels dug, and pumps installed to keep the whole thing dry. The photograph taken on the Davis claim in 1868 by the outstanding Barkerville photographer, Frederick Dally, shows how large wheels turned by water running through a flume were used to drive the pumps.

The Davis claim was estimated to have

yielded $350,000 worth of gold. Old Caledonia produced $750,000 while the Cameron Claim, probably the most famous of all, produced one million dollars. During 1863 its yield varied from 120 to 336 ounces a day. Among the many colourful figures in the Cariboo none was more so than "Cariboo Cameron" himself who fulfilled his wife's last wish to be buried at home in Cornwall, Ontario, by taking her body all the way back there from Barkerville in a tin casket filled with alcohol.

1

2

3

29. AMERICAN THREATS

1. Fort Vancouver. By Henry James Warre
2. North American Boundary Commission, 1860-61. Capt. Darrah with zenith telescope and observatory tent at Yalik R. station
3. Stopping of the *Trent*. From *Illustrated London News*, Dec. 7, 1861
4. Volunteers in camp at time of Fenian threat
5. Engine of Welland Railway that took volunteers from St. Catharines to Port Colborne, June 1, 1866, before Battle of Ridgeway
6. "Desperate charge of the Fenians under Col. O'Neil, near Ridgeway Station, June 2, 1866, and total route (*sic*) of the British troops." Lithograph printed in Buffalo, 1869

In the mid-nineteenth century many Americans believed that it was "the fulfillment of our manifest destiny to overspread the continent allotted by Providence for the free development of our yearly multiplying millions." Others sharing the continent had good cause for alarm and the Mexicans to the south and the Indians to the west were indeed to be heavy losers. Even the British dominions, enjoying the support of a powerful mother country, could not rest easy.

The crisis of the 1840's over Oregon, to which both Britain and the United States

had claims, was brought to a head when James K. Polk won the presidential election of 1844 with the slogan "fifty-four forty or fight"—a claim to the whole of Oregon, 54° 40′ being the southern boundary of Russian Alaska. In 1845, the British sent two lieutenants, Warre and Vavasour, across the continent from Canada to examine defensive possibilities in Oregon. Their report cannot have been encouraging but Warre brought back interesting sketches of the region including one of the Hudson's Bay Company headquarters at Fort Vancouver near the

mouth of the Columbia. Eventually a compromise was reached in the Oregon Treaty (1846) which extended the boundary along the 49th parallel to the sea. During the goldrush period, the vital parts of this line were surveyed by Captain Darrah and other members of a joint North American Boundary Commission.

Tension relaxed sufficiently in the early 1850's for the Reciprocity Treaty of 1854 to be successfully negotiated, but it soon revived and with the outbreak of the Civil War it became acute. In November 1861 when two

4

5

6

Confederate representatives were removed from the British steamship *Trent* on the high seas, war seemed about to break out and British North America became uncomfortably aware of its extreme vulnerability.

The post-war period was even more dangerous. From 1866 to 1871 border threats and raids were made by Fenians as part of the Irish independence movement. The strongest attack was that of John O'Neil and 1500 Fenians across the Niagara River on May 31, 1866 with the cutting of the Welland Canal and Railway as their probable objectives.

Regular troops and volunteers were hastily assembled. O'Neil was victorious over a force of the latter at Ridgeway—not fighting, however, as shown in the propaganda lithograph published sometime afterwards by Fenians in Buffalo—and he made his way back safely to the United States. Other raids of less consequence took place and threats were made from the Maritimes to Manitoba. As late as 1870 a determined stand was needed by the Canadians at Eccles Hill in the Eastern Townships to frustrate another O'Neil attack.

1

30. CONFEDERATION. I, THE CONFERENCES

1. Charlottetown Conference: group photograph
2. The Quebec Conference: group photograph
3. Conference room in Westminster Palace Hotel where London Conference met

The idea of a confederation of all British North America had been discussed for many years before it became in the 1860's a matter of urgent political importance. Dangers from the United States, the problems of government in the Hudson's Bay Territories, internal political difficulties in the self-governing colonies especially in the uneasily united Canada—all of these combined to make union more desirable than ever before. Economic advantages were expected as well, particularly by the railways. And the possibility that now existed of building additional railway lines to overcome the geographic barriers that had hitherto separated the colonies from one another offered an answer to what had always been the main argument against confederation.

The confederation conferences that took place in Charlottetown (September 1864), Quebec (October 1864), and London (December 1866) debated and finally agreed upon the terms of what became the British North America Act bringing the Dominion of Canada into existence on July 1, 1867. The conferences served other purposes as well. They gave the general public a wider interest in British North America as a whole and the the problems facing it. In particular they brought together major political leaders from the various colonies initiating in many cases relationships that would last a lifetime and be of vital importance to the success of the new Dominion.

Among these leaders, there were a number of truly remarkable men. Outstanding in the Canadian delegation were John A. Macdonald, the astute convivial master of political manoeuvre, George Etienne Cartier, the dynamic and experienced spokesman of

French Canada, George Brown, an idealistic but by no means impractical reformer, A. T. Galt, an imaginative financier with wide connections and great negotiating skill, and the eloquent enthusiastic D'Arcy McGee. On a par with these were Samuel Leonard Tilley, the able and thoroughly reliable administrator from New Brunswick, and the energetically aggressive and ambitious Charles Tupper from Nova Scotia. Helpful in the background was the discreetly optimistic governor general, Lord Monck. On the sidelines, but soon to take up the anti-confederation cry was the redoutable Joseph Howe who thought closer association across the ocean with the mother country far more in Nova Scotia's interest than union with an inland Canada.

30. CONFEDERATION.
II, THE PERSONALITIES

1. George Brown, Canada West
2. George Etienne Cartier, Canada East
3. John A. Macdonald, Canada West
4. Joseph Howe, Nova Scotia
5. Thomas D'Arcy McGee, Canada East
6. Alexander Tilloch Galt, Canada East
7. Samuel Leonard Tilley, New Brunswick
8. Charles Tupper, Nova Scotia
9. Lord Monck

2

1

8

7

3

4

5

9

6

67

31. THE RED RIVER INSURRECTION

1. Riel and his Council, autumn 1869

2. Thomas Scott

3. S.S. *International* at Fort Garry

4. William McDougall

5. Fort William

6. John Christian Schultz

7. Adams George Archibald

8. Wolseley expedition crossing portage. By Frances Ann Hopkins who accompanied her husband on the expedition

A major consideration during the Confederation discussions had been the future government of the Hudson's Bay Territories. An expanding Red River settlement was being drawn into closer economic association with St. Paul by the cart trail between them and by Red River steamers such as the *International*. Company rule had, in such circumstances, become anomalous and would probably be followed by annexation to the United States unless union with Canada could be brought about first. Immediately after the new Dominion came into existence therefore the Company and the Canadian and British

governments resumed negotiations and soon agreed on terms for a transfer of authority to take place late in 1869. William McDougall was named the first Canadian governor, but when he arrived at the border on October 30 he found his authority challenged by Métis rebellion.

The negotiators in far-off London had failed to take into account the fears and uncertainties of the inhabitants of the settlement and in particular those of the largest group, the Métis. These saw their semi-nomadic way of life and even their language and religion threatened by a union which would almost

certainly lead to an influx of farmers and of grasping Canadian adventurers, like John Christian Schultz and others, already in the settlement and clearly expecting the change to give them its leadership.

Métis resistance was at first spontaneous. Gradually Louis Riel emerged as leader of a provisional government which, teetering on the brink of violence all winter, conducted negotiations with Donald A. Smith and others sent out from Canada and eventually reached an agreement that would lead to the peaceful entry of the Northwest Territories and a new province of Manitoba into Confederation

under an experienced and conciliatory lieutenant-governor, Adams G. Archibald of Nova Scotia.

Meanwhile, however, Riel had made one tragic mistake. He had given way to his emotions, never under firm control, and had ordered the execution of Thomas Scott. Scott, along with others of Schultz's Canadian party, had behaved with arrogant hostility toward the Métis. A violent young Ontario Orangeman Scott had been particularly and inexcusably provocative. Nevertheless a more experienced and mature leader—Riel was only twenty-five—would have avoided taking

the extreme action that immediately aroused Ontario, made it necessary for the Canadian government to send out *via* Fort William a strong military expedition under Wolseley to ensure recognition of Canadian authority, and would continue for many years to embitter English-French relations throughout Canada.

32. ROUNDING OUT CONFEDERATION.
I, BRITISH COLUMBIA

1. Amor de Cosmos (born William Alexander Smith)
2. New Westminster in the 1860's. F. G. Claudet photograph
3. Nanaimo, 1872
4. Royal Naval Vessels in Esquimalt Harbour in the 1860's. R. Maynard photograph

By 1865, when the Cariboo Road was completed, the height of the gold rush was over and British Columbia was left with heavy debts and a dwindling population. Its capital, the vaunted "Royal City" of New Westminster, remained unfinished in a raw clearing on the banks of the Fraser. On Vancouver Island the situation was much the same except for one bright spot. Esquimalt had just been chosen the North Pacific base of the British fleet raising the hopes of Nanaimo's coalminers and the Island's farmers; but Victoria was an unhappy centre of quarrelling politicians and warehouses bulging with unsalable miners' supplies.

How in these circumstances to avoid complete economic collapse was much debated before decisions were reached in 1866 to unite Vancouver Island with British Columbia and then in 1870 to seek a wider union with Canada. Largely instrumental in bringing about both was the ardently persuasive but erratic Amor de Cosmos. That he was not, as would have been expected, chosen to be one of the delegates sent to Ottawa to negotiate an agreement seems to have been owing to distrust of his personal ambitions. Instead three able, experienced and more solid politicians were selected, J. S. Helmcken, J. W. Trutch, and R. W. W. Carrall. The terms offered these by the Canadians, which included the building of a transcontinental railroad, far exceeded their highest expectations—and those of the rest of British Columbia—with the result that they were speedily accepted and British Columbia became Canada's sixth province on July 20, 1871.

33. ROUNDING OUT CONFEDERATION.
II, THE MARITIMES

1. Intercolonial Railway windmill water tank at Oxford, Nova Scotia
2. Intercolonial Railway Bridge being built over the Miramichi, September 19, 1874
3. Old Intercolonial Railway Station, Saint John, New Brunswick
4. Boats used to cross ice and water from Prince Edward Island in winter

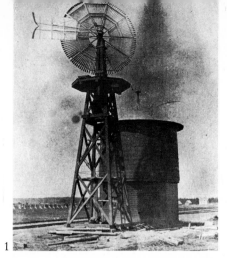

Meanwhile failure of Prince Edward Island to join Confederation remained a nagging problem for the Canadian government. It placed obstacles in the way of enforcing customs and fisheries regulations and left open the possibility of dangerous American encroachments. It was not until 1873 that the Island's stubborn isolationism eventually broke down under the weight of financial pressures particularly in connection with an old problem, that of the absentee proprietors who still owned much of the land, and a new one arising from the unexpectedly heavy expense of the govern-

ment's railway program. An agreement was reached, therefore, under which Canada would help buy out the proprietors, give other specific financial assistance, take over the railway, and guarantee continuous communications with the mainland — this latter being something not previously enjoyed without hazard in winter. Prince Edward Island entered Confederation in July 1, 1873.

While the new obligations to Prince Edward Island were being entered upon, Sandford Fleming as engineer-in-chief was building the Intercolonial Railway promised Nova Scotia

and New Brunswick in the original Confederation agreement. His greatest success was in persuading the government to allow him to build all but three of the bridges of iron, something not previously done in Canada except by the Grank Trunk Railway. When completed in 1876, the main line stretched 562 miles from Halifax to Rivière du Loup where it linked with the Grand Trunk; there were a number of branch lines as well.

2

3

1

TREATY OF WASHINGTON, 1871

In 1871 with the signing of the Treaty of Washington, British and Canadian relations with the United States began a long but not unvarying trend towards improvement, during which traditional hostility would gradually be transformed into traditional friendship. This in itself made the treaty a major event in Canadian history. It was important for more specific reasons as well.

The fact that a Canadian cabinet minister, John A. Macdonald, the Prime Minister, served for the first time as a British representa- tive in negotiations with a foreign power marked a significant step forward in the direction of Canadian control over her own diplomatic relations. Some of the terms of the treaty were also of great interest to Canada. One provided for the opening of the Canadian fisheries to American fishermen for twelve years in return for monetary compensation later set at $5,500,000.00. Another accepted arbitration in the San Juan dispute—Britain and the United States had had troops facing each other since 1859 on that small island that both claimed between Vancouver Island and the mainland. The award of the German Emperor went in 1872 to the United States. Reciprocally free navigation of certain boun- dary waters was also agreed upon, but Canada failed to get two things she particularly wanted: a reciprocity treaty and compensation for damages done by the Fenians. These blows were somewhat softened by Britain's promises to guarantee a Canadian government loan of £2,500,000 much needed because of the railway offered British Columbia the year before—but, even so, a hard-fought struggle took place before ratification by the Canadian Parliament was secured.

4

5

6

HER MAJESTY'S NORTH AMERICAN AND THE
UNITED STATES NORTHERN BOUNDARY COM-
MISSION

The Plains section of the international
boundary between the Lake of the Woods and
the Rockies, where increasing numbers of
traders and settlers were already to be found,
was surveyed by British and American
boundary commissions working jointly during
three seasons beginning in 1872. These commissions were not only models of international
co-operation but, being the first large-scale
expeditions into the region, they served

incidentally to make it better known and to
open it up for further development. The size
and nature of the two expeditions which were
much the same can be judged by the fact that
the British included a company of Royal
Engineers, a corps of mainly Métis scouts, and
some 300 Canadian and British civilians. To
supply these numbers, the wagon trains had to
keep moving all summer from the main depot
at Fort Dufferin on the Red River. The
experience gained by the boundary commission was to prove of immediate value to the
United States Army and the North West
Mounted Police as they began their attempt on

their respective sides of the border and in their
different ways to preserve order amongst the
increasingly restless prairie tribes.

1

2

34. EARLY TRANSCONTINENTAL SURVEYS AND
THE PACIFIC SCANDAL

1. Members of Sandford Fleming's transcontinental survey party, 1872. Fleming
second from left

2. A survey camp on the North Saskatchewan, September 1871. By Charles
Horetzky

3. Sir Hugh Allan. By Robert Harris

4. Alexander Mackenzie

5. "Whither are we drifting?" August, 1873.
By J.W. Bengough

Although the boundary commissions were
the largest individual expeditions in the
prairies in the 1870's, a considerably more
extensive and difficult survey was being
undertaken at the same time by Sandford
Fleming, now engineer-in-chief to the Canadian government. Under his direction, on
July 20, 1871, the day of British Columbia's
entry into Confederation, survey parties began
working eastward from Victoria and westward from the Upper Ottawa seeking the
best route for the promised transcontinental
railway. The first progress report was presented
to the House of Commons in April 1872.

On July 1 of that year, the fifth anniversary
of Confederation, Sandford Fleming himself
started westward from Halifax inspecting as
he went along the Intercolonial Railway, the
construction of which was still his responsibility, and then during the rest of the summer
making a personal examination of the proposed line all the way from the head of Lake
Superior to the Pacific Ocean. The surveys
continued year after year and became more
and more detailed. By the end of 1879 they
had cost over three million dollars.

Meanwhile in 1872 the organization of a
company to build the railway was prepared

These hands are clean!

SEND ME ANOTHER $10,000

PROROGATION AND SUPPRESSION OF THE INVESTIGATION

CANADA

WHITHER ARE WE DRIFTING?

3

4

for by passage of an act of the Canadian Parliament offering aid in the form of land grants and subsidies to a maximum of 50,000,000 acres and $30,000,000. Immediately afterwards, two other acts chartered two rival companies, the Interoceanic and the Canadian Pacific centring respectively around D. L. Macpherson of Toronto and Hugh Allan of Montreal. The latter with his Allan Line of Oceanic Steamships and other enterprises was the stronger financially but was distrusted because of his connections with Americans interested in the Northern Pacific Railway. Macdonald, anxious in any case to avoid

giving an exclusive advantage to either Toronto or Montreal, made every effort to bring the two groups together and to persuade Allan to drop his American associations. Failing in this, he finally brought a third group together which included men from both the former groups (but not Macpherson) and had Allan again as President. This third company was chartered as a new Canadian Pacific Railway Company in February 1873.

In April the whole thing was nullified by the Pacific Scandal. Opponents of the government were able to show that during

the election of the previous summer Allan had made huge contributions to Conservative campaign funds, some of the money even coming from his American associates. Macdonald himself on one occasion had sent an urgent request for more—another $10,000! Macdonald's claim that no corruption was involved in accepting money for electioneering failed to save him—his protest "these hands are clean" was turned into a mockery—and on November 5 the government was brought down.

1

2

3

35. THE INDIANS OF THE PLAINS

1. Camp of Big Bear, chief of Plains Cree Indians, 1883
2. Blackfoot encampment
3. Cree Indians with horse travois and tipis
4. Buffalo herd
5. Crowfoot
6. Crowfoot and family
7. Sitting Bull

In the early 1870's, with the arrival of the boundary commissions, railway surveyors, long creaking wagon trains, and increasing numbers of private traders, life on the plains began to acquire a new tempo. For centuries it had been characterized by the slow seasonal migratory movement north and south of scattered Indian tribes following the vast herds of buffalo on which their livelihood depended. The introduction of horses and firearms in the mid-eighteenth century had greatly raised standards of living but without altering the old rhythm. Horse travois that doubled as tipi poles could carry more than the earlier dog travois, and mounted and armed men had obvious advantages over the powerful but awkward buffalo.

All changed disastrously in the 1870's and within a generation the tribes would be decimated by disease, starvation and war and the buffalo would be gone. The destruction of the buffalo in a brief decade or so is a principal event in North American history. Some 5000 hunters and skinners exclusive of the Indians were estimated to have been at work annually among the herds, and millions of buffalo robes were shipped east by rail and river steamer. In 1876 alone, the famous I. G. Baker wagon trains carried south from Fort Macleod to Fort Benton, Montana, at the head of steam navigation on the Missouri, 40,000 buffalo robes and as many wolf pelts. By the mid-1880's the slaughter was over and the Indians, having no other recourse, were being herded disconsolately into reservations by the United States Army and the North West Mounted Police.

There were differences in the way it was done north and south of the border, as is

76

4

5
6

7

shown in what happened to the Sioux and the Blackfoot and their leaders, Sitting Bull and Crowfoot. In June 1876 Sitting Bull's Sioux, long victimized by corrupt Indian agents and greedy frontier interests, defeated and killed Colonel George A. Custer and 265 men of the United States Army. A few months later many made their way across the Canadian border where Superintendent J. M. Walsh and a North West Mounted Police patrol kept them under peaceful surveillance until they could be persuaded to move south again in 1881 after long negotiations with the United States government. Meanwhile, a little over a year after Custer's "last stand" and while bitter warfare was still raging in the American west Crowfoot and other chiefs of the powerful Blackfoot confederacy took part in colourful ceremonies that marked the signing of Treaty Number Seven giving up general territorial rights in return for specified reservations together with financial and other aid.

1 2

3

36. THE WHISKY TRADERS AND THE NORTH WEST MOUNTED POLICE

1. Fort Edmonton, 1871. By C. Horetzky
2. I. G. Baker store, Fort Macleod, 1879
3. Fort Walsh, 1878
4. Wagon trains leaving Fort Benton, 1878
5. Police inspecting traders' carts, 1874. By Henri Julien
6. Fort Macleod polo team, 1890
7. James Farquharson Macleod
8. Fort Whoop-Up, interior
9. Fort Whoop-Up with U.S. flag
10. Mounted police in early uniforms and forage caps

4 5

There were a number of reasons for the remarkable success of small North West Mounted Police patrols in dealing with Sitting Bull and the whole shifting population of some 30,000 Indians on the Canadian prairies during the time when bitter warfare was still the rule just across the border. The absolute courage and fairness displayed by the original officers, especially Macleod and Walsh, was of course an indispensable factor. The tradition of order and mutual confidence inherited from the days of Hudson's Bay Company rule and from colonial campaigns in which red-coated British soldiers had fought side by side with their Indian allies was important as well. So too was the fact that the force became operational in time— before frontier greed could produce the anarchy that it had to the south.

The manner in which the police took up their duties did much also to enhance their effectiveness. 275 men under Commissioner French and Assistant Commissioner Macleod set forth in a body from the Red River on July 9, 1874, to make a great initial sweep through the prairies that would take them as far as the foothills of the Rockies. With its uniformed men and officers, 339 horses, 142 draft oxen, 93 cattle, 114 Red River carts, 73 wagons, 20 Métis drivers, two nine-pounder guns, two brass mortars, assorted mowing machines, portable forges and field kitchens, and with the well-known cartoonist Henri Julien to serve as correspondent for the *Canadian Illustrated News*, it was an impressive expedition and one that would attract considerable attention both on the prairies and back east where Canadians knew little as yet about their vast western territories.

6

7

8

10

9

Some weeks out one troop broke off and took well-used trails northwestward to the Hudson's Bay Company's main North Saskatchewan centre, Fort Edmonton, establishing headquarters there. The rest continued westward, some eventually returning by a different route, others under Macleod going on to investigate Fort Whoop-Up and other "whisky forts" built in Blackfoot territory during the past few years by traders from Benton. Fort Macleod hastily constructed in that vicinity in the fall and Fort Walsh erected the next year in the equally notorious Cypress Hills effectively ended the whisky trade and led to cordial relations being established with Crowfoot and other grateful Blackfoot and Cree chieftains. Legal trade with Benton continued, of course. The trail between it and Fort Macleod remained the principal trade route of the region until the coming of the Canadian Pacific Railway, and from the beginning the Police themselves were largely dependent on the I. G. Baker Company of Benton and St. Louis.

37. BUILDING THE CANADIAN PACIFIC RAILWAY

1. William Van Horne
2. Stoney Creek bridge, 1885
3. Steam shovel
4. Saloon at Donald, B.C., 1884
5. Coolie labour, 1884
6. *Butcher's Boy*, C.P.R. supply vessel on Lake Superior
7. George Stephen
8. Laying track
9. Red Sucker Trestle north of Lake Superior
10. Corry Brothers' tunnel, B.C., 1884
11. Dougherty's Cut north of Lake Superior
12. Landing of *Countess of Dufferin* at Winnipeg, 1877

2

1

3

6

5

4

The Pacific Scandal and an economic depression of the same year ended any immediate hope of organizing a private company to build a transcontinental railway. Alexander Mackenzie who succeeded Macdonald as prime minister in 1873 was obliged to begin work upon it therefore as a government undertaking. This policy was continued when Macdonald returned to power in 1878 until he was finally able to bring together a strong financial syndicate headed by George Stephen, President of the Bank of Montreal. A new Canadian Pacific Railway with Stephen as president was chartered in 1881, receiving among other benefits a promise of up to $25,000,000 and 25,000,000 acres of land, the sections of the line already built by the government, and a twenty-year guarantee against other companies being allowed to build connections with American railway systems to the south. Stephen and his associates promised in return the completion of a through line by May 31, 1891.

This agreement was as successful as the earlier one negotiated with Allan had been disastrous. William Van Horne, an experienced railwayman, was appointed general manager and brought with him as general purchasing agent, Thomas Shaughnessy. The organizing ability of Van Horne, the energy and persuasiveness of Shaughnessy, and the financial skill of Stephen, together with the support given him by his cousin Donald A. Smith and by the Macdonald government, combined to result in the last spike being driven on November 7, 1885—over five years earlier than had originally been promised or deemed at all feasible.

The greatest difficulties had been en-

8

7

9

10

11

12

countered in the mountains of British Columbia and the rough hills and muskeg north of Lake Superior. They had been energetically overcome by building high trestle bridges, tunnelling with recently invented dynamite, and using steam shovels, special track-laying machines, and huge gangs of men, some of them coolies brought in for the purpose from China. To keep each section supplied as it was being built required ingenious use of the railway itself as well as shipping on the Great Lakes and the Pacific and even on the prairie rivers.

THE CANADIAN PACIFIC RAILWAY
DINING CARS
Excel in Elegance of Design and Furniture
AND IN THE
Quality of Food and Attendance
ANYTHING HITHERTO OFFERED TO
TRANSCONTINENTAL TRAVELLERS.

The fare provided is the best procurable, and the cooking has a wide reputation for excellence. Local delicacies, such as trout, prairie hens, antelope steaks, Fraser River salmon, succeed one another as the train moves westward.

The wines are of the Company's special importation, and are of the finest quality.

These cars accompany all transcontinental trains, and are managed directly by the Railway Company, which seeks, as with its hotels and sleeping cars, to provide every comfort and luxury without regard to cost—looking to the general profit of the Railway rather than to the immediate returns from these branches of its service

47

1

FOR the comfort and convenience of settlers going to the CANADIAN NORTH-WEST, the
CANADIAN PACIFIC RAILWAY
PROVIDES A SPECIAL FORM OF PASSENGER EQUIPMENT, KNOWN AS
COLONIST CARS

Which are run through to MANITOBA and BRITISH COLUMBIA on the regular Express Train leaving MONTREAL each week day. They are really "SLEEPING CARS," modelled after the style of the first-class "PULLMAN," with upper and lower berths, closets, lavatories, &c., &c., the only difference being that the seats and berths are not upholstered. Occupants may supply their own bedding, or can purchase of the Company's Agents at QUEBEC, MONTREAL, or TORONTO, a mattress, pillow and blanket for $2.50 (10 shillings), which they can retain at the end of their journey.

The accompanying cut shows the interior of a Colonist Car, with a portion of the berths made up for sleeping purposes.

Holders of COLONIST or SECOND-CLASS TICKETS are allowed FREE USE OF THESE CARS FROM THE BEGINNING TO THE END OF THEIR JOURNEY OVER THE CANADIAN PACIFIC RAILWAY.

2

3

38. THE C.P.R. IN OPERATION.
I, TRANSCONTINENTAL PASSENGER SERVICES

1. Dining car advertisement, 1888
2. Back cover of C.P.R. immigration booklet on Manitoba, 1888
3. Arrival of first transcontinental passenger train at Port Moody, July 4, 1886
4. Arrival of first transcontinental passenger train at Vancouver, May 23, 1887
5. Some C.P.R. rail fares in 1888

After the last spike was driven on November 7, 1885, the special train carrying the dignitaries concerned went on to Port Moody, completing the continental crossing from Montreal in five days running time at an average speed of 24 miles per hour. Months of work were still needed, however, to bring the line and equipment up to the standards required for day-in day-out service. It was not until June 28, 1886, therefore, that the first transcontinental passenger train complete with colonist cars, first-class coaches, a diner, and two luxurious parlour and sleeping cars left

Montreal to the cheers of the assembled crowd and a fifteen-gun salute. It arrived at Port Moody, having dropped off some cars *en route*, on July 4 and the first lady passenger was presented with a bouquet of flowers and had her picture taken.

The rejoicing at Port Moody on what would otherwise have been an entirely auspicious occasion was shadowed by knowledge that twelve miles farther west on Burrard Inlet its rival, incorporated as Vancouver in April and undaunted by a disastrous fire in June, was preparing feverishly to become the

4

5

new western terminus of the railroad. Vancouver had what Port Moody lacked, an easily accessible deep-water harbour, and this was essential to a railway already busily engaged in extending its operations across the Pacific by means of steamship services. On May 23, 1887, the eve of the Queen's Birthday, the first through passenger train, running over still unballasted ties but gaily decorated, arrived at Vancouver's docks and was enthusiastically greeted by the city's first mayor and almost all of its inhabitants.

FIRST-CLASS SLEEPING AND PARLOR CAR TARIFF.

FOR ONE LOWER OR ONE UPPER BERTH IN SLEEPING CAR BETWEEN

Quebec and Montreal......$1.50	Pt. Arthur & Vancouver.$15.00	Boston and Montreal......$2.00
Montreal and Toronto......2.00	Toronto and Chicago........3.00	New York and Montreal....2.00
Montreal and Winnipeg....8.00	Toronto and Detroit........2.00	Chicago and St. Paul.......2.00
Montreal and Vancouver..20.00	Toronto and Winnipeg......8.00	St. Paul and Winnipeg......3.00
Ottawa and Toronto........2.00	Toronto and Vancouver...18.50	St. Paul and Vancouver...13.50
Ottawa and Vancouver ...20.00		Winnipeg and Vancouver.12.00

FOR ONE SEAT IN PARLOR CAR BETWEEN

Quebec and Montreal......$0.75	Montreal and Toronto....$1.00	Toronto and Owen Sound.$0.50
Three Rivers and Montreal .50	Ottawa and Toronto........1.00	Toronto and St. Thomas.... .50
Montreal and Ottawa...... .50	Peterboro' and Toronto..... .25	Toronto and Detroit.........1.00

Between other stations rates are in proportion. Accommodation in First-Class Sleeping Cars and in Parlor Cars will be sold only to holders of First-Class transportation.

38. THE C.P.R. IN OPERATION.
II, THE PACIFIC STEAMSHIPS

1. *Empress of China* leaving Vancouver, 1903
2. C.P.R. Railway Station and Wharf, Vancouver, 1899
3. S.S. *Parthia*, c. 1887
4. Unloading tea from S.S. *Parthia*, c. 1887

1

2

From the beginning George Stephen had realized that local traffic could not support a railway running, as the Canadian Pacific Railway would for many years at least, through vast territories sparsely if at all settled. The company would have instead to rely heavily on becoming part of a world transportation system carrying goods and passengers from the rapidly opening Orient through to the eastern seaboard of North America and on to Britain and Europe. For the time being he was satisfied to rely on other carriers to handle the traffic of the Atlantic section. On the Pacific, however, in order for

Vancouver to become the rival of San Francisco and Tacoma and draw traffic from the Suez Canal, the Canadian Pacific Railway would have to have its own steamships. It would have the advantage in acquiring them of a claim to imperial support in that they and the railway could in case of need serve as a major part of a British military route to India less liable to interference than that already existing through the Mediterranean and the Suez.

Discussions along these lines were begun by Stephen well before the railway itself was completed. At the time of the first Colonial

Conference in 1887 concrete proposals were made for a mail subsidy in support of a regular service between Hong Kong and Vancouver *via* Yokohama to be provided by steamships of a certain standard and capable of transformation into armed cruisers. Two years later, on July 15, 1889, a ten-year contract along these lines was finally signed providing for an imperial subsidy of £45,000 a year and a Canadian of £15,000.

Meanwhile back in 1886 preliminary support for Stephen's arguments had been provided by the arrival of the clipper *W. B. Flint* at Port Moody from Yokohama with a cargo of tea

3

4

and the dispatch of a ten-car tea train for Montreal to establish a record for fast freight between Japan and eastern North America. In 1887, three steamships, the *Abyssinia*, the *Parthia*, and the *Batavia*, were chartered to begin the Hong Kong–Vancouver run. The first of these, the *Abyssinia*, entered Vancouver with tea, passengers, and a pioneer shipment of silk on June 14 only three weeks after the arrival of the first transcontinental from Montreal. On the signing of the mail contract in 1889, orders were placed for three new larger and faster vessels, the sleek clipper-stemmed *Empress of Japan*, *Empress of India*, and *Empress of China*. These replaced the chartered ships on the run in 1891 and their success was ensured by highly effective arrangements for the conduct of the company's business made by T. G. Shaughnessy during a four-month stay in Japan and China shortly afterwards. The *Empresses* not only operated profitably all through the 1890's but there can be little doubt but that the trade they brought from the East played an important role in helping the Canadian Pacific Railway survive the panic of 1893 and the following depression that brought bankruptcy to so many American lines.

38. THE C.P.R. IN OPERATION.
     III, THE IMPROVEMENT AND EXTENSION OF
     SERVICES

1. The St. Lawrence Bridge at Lachine.
    Cantilever span under construction, March
    4, 1887
2. St. Lawrence Bridge. Divers at no. 13
    caisson, Oct. 11, 1886
3. C.P.R. locomotives blocking Northern
    Pacific right-of-way
4. C.P.R. docks and elevator at Port Arthur
5. S.S. *Athabasca* in Port Arthur, *c.* 1885
6. Dam at Bassano, Alberta

7. H.B.C. store and C.P.R. Land Office at
    Battleford
8. Vancouver Hotel, 1889
9. Chateau Frontenac at Quebec, *c.* 1901

The creation of through steamship and rail
services from Hong Kong *via* Vancouver to
Montreal was only part of what had to be
done to ensure the Canadian Pacific Railway's
successful operation. Numerous branch lines
had to be built and access had to be obtained
to winter ports in the Maritimes and New
England. In this latter connection a key factor
was the building of the St. Lawrence Bridge

at Lachine to compete with the Grand Trunk
Railway's Victoria Bridge. Apart from the
Grand Trunk, the Canadian Pacific's most
dangerous competitor was the Northern
Pacific in the prairie region. Competition
there was supposed to have been eliminated by
the "monopoly clause" in the 1881 charter.
This had been abandoned, however, under
pressure from Manitoba and in return for a
much needed loan guarantee, and the Northern
Pacific had even succeeded in crossing the
Canadian Pacific's line in several places despite
vigorous resistance including at one stage the
use of locomotives.

Grain elevators, lake steamships, and hotels

5

6

7

8

9

were all important auxiliaries to the rail service and in many cases were provided by the Canadian Pacific Railway itself. Van Horne, who had an enthusiastic interest in good living and in art and landscape, concerned himself personally with the hotels not only at key centres like Quebec and Vancouver but in the mountains of British Columbia and Alberta where he believed a major tourist industry could be developed. He employed Bruce Price, a leading American architect, and worked closely with him in the building of the Banff Springs Hotel and the Chateau Frontenac at Quebec. The latter set the pattern for the chateau-style architecture for which the

Canadian Pacific Railway hotels became known.

The land-grant clause in its charter made the Canadian Pacific Railway from the beginning a land as well as a transportation company. Promotion of immigration was vital to both of these interests and was actively undertaken. Coal on some of its lands, and particularly on that acquired as a result of the 1897 agreement to build a line through the Crow's Nest Pass, attracted the company into coal mining and it operated for a time the smelter at Trail as well. In 1903 when the Canadian government was trying to wind up all railway land grant arrangements it persuaded the Canadian

Pacific Railway to take as part of the land still owing it a large semi-arid block in southern Alberta for opening up by means of extensive irrigation. When the Bassano dam was ready for use in 1914 the company had completed what was at that time the greatest irrigation development on the continent.

1

2

39. THE NORTHWEST REBELLION.
I, PERSONALITIES

1. Interior of Fort Pitt just before the Rebellion: group of Cree Indians including Big Bear (5) and one of his sons (2); Angus McKay (6), Hudson's Bay Company trader; N.W.M.P. Corporal R. B. Sleigh (12), killed shortly afterwards during fighting at Cut Knife Creek on Poundmaker's reserve. Fort Pitt had to be abandoned in April under threats from Big Bear and was looted and burned

2. Métis leaders in handcuffs after Rebellion

3. Gabriel Dumont after the Rebellion when he had become a member of "Buffalo Bill" Cody's Wild West show

4. Father Albert Lacombe, the great Oblate missionary, respected throughout the plains where he founded churches and schools and was largely influential in preventing the Blackfoot tribes from interfering with the building of the Canadian Pacific Railway and from joining the Northwest Rebellion

5. Captured Indian leaders Big Bear (seated, second from left) with his youngest son, Horse Child, beside him, and Poundmaker (seated right); N.W.M.P. Superintendent R. B. Deane (centre rear) with Father Louis Cochin on his right and Father Alexis André, the parish priest at Prince Albert on his left

The North West Mounted Police had been remarkably successful in maintaining order on the plains during the great changes that followed the disappearance of the buffalo herds and accompanied the intrusion of the Canadian Pacific Railway and the beginning of settlement. Pressures began to build up,

4

3

5

however, in the 1880's when the railway became a visible fact and when the full difficulty of an adjustment to the new way of life began to be felt. Indian unrest increased and there were signs that Big Bear who had long been reluctant to settle on a reservation was hoping in association with Poundmaker and other dissatisfied Cree chiefs to bring about a confederacy that could wrest better terms from the Canadian government.

At least as serious were the problems of the Métis and the English-speaking half-breeds many of whom had left the Red River to find new homes in the plains, especially in the valley of the South Saskatchewan. Lacking even the treaty guarantees given to the Indians and rebuffed by a surprisingly insensitive Canadian government, they began to think in terms of another List of Rights like that drafted during the Red River Rebellion and of inviting Louis Riel from his Montana exile to help them present it.

1

2

3

4

5

39. THE NORTHWEST REBELLION,
    II, THE FIGHTING

1. The telegraph station, Humboldt, 1883
2. Middleton's troops en route through Touchwood Hills to Humboldt, 1885
3. S.S. *Northcote* before being damaged at Batoche
4. "Gun pit." Photograph by Capt. J. Peters
5. "Shelling Batoche, last shot before the attack on the guns." By Capt. Peters
6. "He shot Capt. French." By Capt. Peters
7. "Sewing up the dead." By Capt. Peters

8. General Middleton and wounded aides. By Capt. Peters
9. Riel a prisoner. By Capt. Peters

Riel and his family made the long journey northward over the trails from Montana to Batoche in the heart of the South Saskatchewan Métis country during the summer of 1884. The following winter, conferences were held and committees set up, not only among the Métis and English-speaking half-breeds but including white settlers as well, to discuss real or imaginary grievances against the government in Ottawa. Caught up in the excitement, Riel began to lose his emotional balance. His mind became dominated by increasingly extreme and peculiar religious ideas. Moderates drew away from him but the simple, superstitious majority were stimulated by his very fervour and came to share it. On March 19, 1885, along with Gabriel Dumont who would provide the real leadership, Riel proclaimed a provisional government. A week later, on March 26, violence began with the defeat of a small militia and police force at Duck Lake. By April 2 it had spread to the Indians, Big Bear's Crees massacring whites including two priests at Frog Lake.

8

6

7

9

Telegraph lines, first strung across the prairies in the late 1870's, had kept the government informed of what was threatening, and militia and police forces were already being hastily gathered under Major General Middleton. Van Horne was ready too to assist—and to seize the excellent opportunity of stressing the national value of the Canadian Pacific Railway. With experience in the movement of troops going back to Civil War days and all of his tremendous energy, he was able to move men, guns, and equipment rapidly westward bridging the few remaining gaps in the line by using sleighs and wagons. Within days of the Frog Lake massacre a main

force under Middleton began marching northward from the railway at Qu'Appelle toward Batoche 200 miles away, a second under Lieutenant Colonel Otter moved from Swift Current toward Battleford, and a third under General Strange from Calgary toward Edmonton.

Middleton advanced cautiously as he entered the Métis country, but finally reached Batoche on May 9. His intention was to attack not only by land but from the *Northcote* used as a gunboat on the river. The *Northcote* after a premature attack, however, withdrew partially disabled before the main four-day bombardment began. Participating in this,

and photographing it as well, was Captain James Peters of "A" Battery Royal Canadian Artillery. Batoche was taken on May 12, and three days later Riel was captured.

Meanwhile, Otter had successfully relieved Battleford but had been checked by Poundmaker at Cut Knife Hill on May 2. Middleton advancing to his assistance received Poundmaker's surrender on May 26. Farther west, Strange after reaching Edmonton and moving down the North Saskatchewan was stopped at Frenchmen's Butte by Big Bear and it was not until July 2 that the latter finally surrendered, bringing the Rebellion to an end.

39. THE NORTHWEST REBELLION.
    III, THE AFTERMATH

1. The Riel jurymen
2. Riel on trial. Photograph by O. B. Buell
3. Arch over Main St., Winnipeg, welcoming home Middleton's troops
4. Welcome at Owen Sound of C.P.R. steamships with returning volunteers
5. Indian Commissioner David Laird explaining terms of Treaty No. 8 at Fort Vermilion 1899
6. Chipewyan chief Maurice Piche who accepted Treaty No. 8 at Fond du Lac, 1899
7. Métis meeting at Fort Dunvegan, 1899
8. Legislative Council of the Northwest Territories, 1885

For the militia volunteers, the end of the Rebellion meant a speedy return home to a hero's welcome and the offer of a free two-quarter-section homestead in the West or Dominion land scrip worth $80. For the rebels, who like Gabriel Dumont, managed to escape to the United States, it meant years of wandering exile. For those captured, it meant trials in Regina followed by imprisonment and in a few cases execution. Poundmaker and Big Bear, shown to have been pushed reluctantly into actual violence by their young men whose passions they had helped to rouse, were let off with light prison sentences. Riel

however was found guilty of high treason and sentenced to death. On November 16, after a special commission had concluded that he was not insane, he was hanged. This, like the execution of Thomas Scott fifteen years earlier, stirred the emotions of French- and English-speaking Canadians and embittered their relations with one another to an extent few other events in Canadian history have done.

In the West itself, the Rebellion's aftermath included further efforts to prepare not only the Indians but now also the Métis for the inevitable beginning of an agricultural

5

6

7

8

economy. The policy of negotiating treaties with the Indians as civilization approached and helping them settle on reservations was continued and the machinery for making it effective was strengthened. And now, along with the Indian agents there went Half-Breed Scrip Commissioners to explain a new policy the government had been forced by the Rebellion to adopt.

Scrip was negotiable paper entitling the holder to quarter sections of available crown land. It was offered to the Northwest volunteers as it would be to those who went to South Africa, both as a reward and as an inducement to go west. Its main use, however, was in meeting Métis claims. The Manitoba Act (1870) had recognized these, in so far as the Manitoba Métis were concerned, by setting aside 1,400,000 acres for their use. After much difficulty it had been decided to allot this on the basis of 240 acres to each child and scrip for 160 acres to each head of family. The scrip had all too frequently been frittered away by the Métis and found its way cheaply into the hands of land speculators.

Claims of Saskatchewan Métis to similar land and scrip had been resisted by the government up to the time of the Rebellion on the ground that if they really wanted land they could now get it like anyone else by complying with the terms of the Free Homestead Act of 1872. This argument, while superficially sound, failed to acknowledge the Métis' special claims on account of their Indian ancestry and it was not accompanied by positive assistance in overcoming the real difficulties they were having in adjusting to their changing circumstances. After the Rebellion, therefore, scrip was introduced into the Northwest Territories. Despite all efforts at explanation and warning, the results were much the same as they had been in Manitoba.

1

40. PRAIRIE SETTLEMENT. I, ARRIVALS

1. Immigrants on board *Empress of Britain*, *c.* 1911
2. Arrival of first Mennonites at Winnipeg, July 31, 1874
3. Americans arriving from South Dakota, 1891
4. Americans arriving in southern Alberta, *c.* 1893
5. Clifford Sifton
6. Dominion Lands rush at Prince Albert court house, *c.* 1909

When immigration into the prairies began in the 1870's and 1880's, it was largely from Ontario and the United Kingdom. It included, however, a few non-English-speaking groups foreshadowing the influx of the next two decades. Two groups of special interest were the Mennonites and the Icelanders. Between 1874 and 1878, three whole communities of Mennonites totalling some 7500 people were transferred from the Russian Ukraine to Manitoba after reaching an agreement with the Canadian government guaranteeing religious freedom and exemption from military service. The first Icelanders settled at Gimli on

Lake Winnipeg in 1875 and were followed during the next twenty years by some 10,000 others scattering westward across the plains and into British Columbia. Settlement on the whole remained, however, disappointingly slow until the later 1890's when a boom began that would last until 1913.

The change coincided with the coming to power of Wilfred Laurier's Liberal Government in 1896 and the appointment of Clifford Sifton as minister of the interior. Sifton had himself gone West as a young man and he now undertook to promote its settlement with all his tremendous energy and organizing

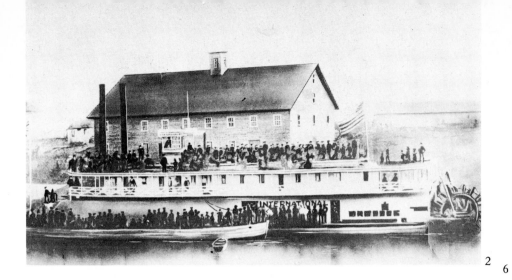

2

6

5

3

4

ability. He re-organized the notoriously inefficient Department of the Interior, established immigration agencies in Britain and the United States, and became particularly known for his active and successful seeking of central European immigrants through an organization of steamship and booking agents, the North Atlantic Trading Company of Hamburg. The population of the prairies, about 250,000 in 1891, rose to 420,000 by 1901 and to over 800,000 by 1906, the year following Sifton's resignation. The influx, now at its height, continued and by 1911 the prairie population exceeded 1,300,000.

Sifton's efforts were by no means solely responsible for the transformation that had taken place. The Canadian Pacific Railway, numerous colonization companies, and private individuals all supplemented the work of the government in promoting immigration. Moreover, for the first time world conditions were becoming favourable for the settlement of the Canadian prairies. In the United Kingdom and Western Europe urban and industrial growth was creating a rapidly expanding market for wheat. In the United States, on the other hand, the West was beginning to fill up and Americans themselves were turning to "the

last best West" north of the 49th parallel. In 1897, they had made up only 11 per cent of total Canadian immigration as compared with 52 per cent from the British Isles. By 1902 the corresponding percentages were 39 and 26, and in 1910 a peak was reached when just about half of all immigrants were Americans.

1

3

4

40. PRAIRIE SETTLEMENT. II, THE DOUKHOBORS

1. Friends of the Doukhobors including Leo Tolstoy (standing, left)
2. Mealtime on S.S. *Lake Huron* en route to Canada, 1899
3. Threshing grain with flails
4. Marching from Yorkton, spring, 1899
5. Women pulling plough
6. Peter Veregin in England *en route* to Canada, 1902
7. Village of Vosnesenya, Thunder Hill Colony
8. Doukhobors leaving Yorkton on way to British Columbia, 1909

The Doukhobor migration of 1899 was the largest of a number of similar transfers of whole communities from Europe to new villages on the Canadian prairies, villages they tried to make as much like those they had left behind as possible and where they lived more or less segregated from their neighbours and from the Canadian way of life. In the case of the Doukhobors, their segregation was made more complete by their extreme religious beliefs which included a mystical emphasis on the divinity of the individual and refusal to acknowledge governmental authority.

The Doukhobors, like the Mennonites before them, wanted to leave Russia for a land where they could enjoy religious freedom and be exempt from governmental interference, particularly the requirement of military service. Severe persecutions in the 1890's aroused widespread sympathy. Among those who urged Canada to provide a refuge were the famous Russian novelist Count Leo Tolstoy and influential Quakers in both the United States and Britain. Tolstoy gave special

6

5

7

8

assurances that the Doukhobors "were not addicted to outbreaks of fanaticism and that there could be no doubt that they would be law abiding."

Four ships brought a total of over 7400 Doukhobors through the Mediterranean and across the Atlantic to Canada in the spring of 1899. The Canadian Pacific Railway allowed them reduced rates to the end of steel at Yorkton and from there they marched northward across the prairies to the tracts of land set aside for them. That summer, while the women and some men built crude log or clay houses and began to break sod, the rest of the

men sought work on the approaching railway or on established farms in order to earn ready cash. A pattern of work was established that would continue while thriving communities were gradually brought into being.

Peter Veregin, whose succession to the Doukhobor leadership had prompted a religious revival in the late 1880's and a renewal of persecution, was an exile in Siberia when the migration took place and was not able to reach Canada until 1902. The emphasis that he had always placed on communal living was reinforced when he found that the men who had been working outside the villages in the

summers were already drifting from economic orthodoxy. A rift began to deepen between those supporting Veregin's attempt to enforce the old ideal of a communal economy and those preferring economic independence. In 1908 the community-minded followed Veregin to more isolated valleys in southern British Columbia where they could practise their beliefs more readily and where the more extreme—the Sons of Freedom—would constitute a continuing problem for the authorities. Those who remained in Saskatchewan gradually adjusted to the society around them.

1

4

2

5

3

40. PRAIRIE SETTLEMENT. III, HOMESTEADING

1. Barr Colony camp at Saskatoon, 1903
2. The camp barber
3. Home of a Barr colonist, Lloydminster, 1906
4. "This shack was dug out of the hillside Oct. 26, 1910, by me and I lived in it for three winters to prove up with . . . . I was 21 years then." A. Jones
5. House on Bell Farm, Indian Head, Saskatchewan, 1884

6. Log house of John Wood, Erwood, Saskatchewan
7. The Hunter brothers in their house at Dog Pound near Cochrane, Alberta, c. 1897
8. Sod house near Wainwright, Alberta, c. 1911
9. Bob and "Ham" Marshall building their sod house near Coronation
10. Ivan Lupul's Ukrainian house, Wostok, 1902
11. Barn raising at Rolland, Manitoba, 1912

An immigration project widely different from that of the Doukhobors was one conceived by the Rev. I. M. Barr who visited Canada in 1902 and hurried back to England with plans for a colony of English people of means and an agricultural bent. Put forward at a time when interest in Canada was reaching its peak and restless South African war veterans were numerous, Barr's plan was enthusiastically received and the colonists who followed him to Canada in the spring of 1903 were considerably more numerous and varied than he had anticipated. In April, a city of 500 tents

appeared beside the railway tracks at Saskatoon—more the result of government initiative than that of Barr, who was proving himself completely incapable of large-scale organization and who would shortly be replaced by the Rev. G. E. Lloyd, later Bishop of Saskatchewan. Having made what purchases they required, including horses and wagons, the colonists were soon strung out along the 200-mile road to what became Lloydminster, sheltering on the way in large tents erected at intervals by the government. In due course, those who persisted became part of a prosperous agricultural community.

Individuals as well as groups made their way in increasing numbers out on to the prairies. Some had little but strength and courage—like A. Jones who endured much to "prove up" his homestead but lived to see his sons farming it after him. Others like Major W. R. Bell and his associates began immediately on a large scale. The Bell Farm near Indian Head had not only fine houses and a mill but, as early as 1884, 45 binders were working its fields. It also pioneered the use of seed broadcasters.

40. PRAIRIE SETTLEMENT.
    IV, THE WHEAT ECONOMY

1. Buffalo bones
2. Ukrainians digging potatoes
3. "Sod busting" with steam tractors, c. 1909
4. Harvesters at Winnipeg, c. 1900
5. Reaping, 1906
6. A two-horse-power threshing machine, 1905
7. Opening of grain elevator at Kennedy, 1908

The initial cash crop of many a settler, helping pay perhaps for his first plough and seed, was buffalo bones. The prairies were white with them following the great slaughters of the 1870's and huge piles were carted to the nearest railway sidings for shipment to the United States where they would be used in the manufacture of fertilizer, the bleaching of sugar, and various other processes. It is estimated that over 3000 railway carloads left Saskatoon alone, each containing the bones of as many as 250 animals.

On a permanent basis, grain and especially wheat became the crop of the prairies. The great level stretches of fertile soil, the hot summers, and the light rainfall favoured grain growing to such an extent that, except among some of the European peoples with a strong tradition of self-sufficiency, little else was raised even in the early stages. Red Fife wheat, long the standard variety in Ontario, became dominant also on the prairies by the 1880's. A hard red grain with a high protein content, it remained unchallenged for twenty-five years, winning a world-wide reputation for its bread-making qualities. After 1909, it began to be replaced by Marquis developed on Dominion Experimental Farms by Dr. Charles

E. Saunders. Marquis had the advantage of maturing some ten days earlier than Red Fife and being more resistant to certain types of rust.

Wheat production rose with startling rapidity. The total for all of Canada stood at some 40,000,000 bushels in 1897. By 1905, that of the West alone was over 67,000,000 and by 1913 it had risen to 209,000,000. Harvesting in the short and uncertain period between maturity and the first frost was a perennial problem. It required by the early 1900's an annual influx of as many as 25,000 harvesters and encouraged farmers to intro-

duce as rapidly as they could afford them improved binders and threshers, steam tractors, and even some early combines.

The building of grain elevators and the development of rail, lake, and ocean transportation had to keep pace with the growth of the grain trade. From the first, the Canadian Pacific and other railways gave special concessions to those willing to build country elevators and by 1900 these already had a 12,000,000 bushel capacity. The Canadian Pacific Railway itself opened the first terminal elevator at Port Arthur in 1884 and by 1902 the capacity there was 7,500,000 bushels.

2

1

3

40. PRAIRIE SETTLEMENT.

V, RANCHING AND GENERAL PROSPERITY

1 Miss Hazel Walker on Buttons at the Calgary Rodeo (1912), the forerunner of the Stampede

2. "Nigger John" Ware and family: one of the greatest and most popular of Canadian cowboys

3. A roundup in southern Alberta

4. Homestead behind new Rogerson home, near Rolland, Manitoba, 1905

5. Interior of new Rogerson home

The disappearance of the buffalo and the coming of the railway opened the way for ranching in the semi-arid south-western prairies and foothills. Expansion was extremely rapid. In 1881, when the first large-scale ranching venture was commenced by Senator M. H. Cochrane of Compton, Quebec, it was estimated that there were only about 3000 cattle in the whole region. In 1885 a wide sweep made out from Fort Macleod during the greatest roundup that ever took place in Canada brought in 60,000. By 1905 there were over 400,000 and large numbers of horses and sheep as well, despite the encroachments on the range being made by homesteaders.

Almost as rapid was the achievement of solid rural prosperity throughout the whole of the Canadian West. Original homesteads were replaced within a generation by large comfortable homes as fine as their equivalents in old established regions of Ontario and furnished with the same florid late-Victorian elegance. By 1905, when Mr. Rogerson's home was new, fenced fields of waving grain, great herds, and crisscrossing lines of road and railway spread out across the whole of the vast prairies where just thirty years before the buffalo had roamed followed by Indian and half-breed hunters.

4

5

1

2

40. PRAIRIE SETTLEMENT.
VI, INDUSTRIAL AND URBAN DEVELOPMENT

1. Grading a railroad with mules and scoops
2. Sir William Mackenzie
3. Sir Donald Mann
4. Old Pat Burns plant, Calgary, 1910
5. Bob Edwards, editor of the Calgary *Eye Opener*

6. Land office of Northwestern Coal and Navigation Company, Lethbridge, *c.* 1886
7. Sugar factory, Raymond, Alberta, *c.* 1904
8. North-west Irrigation Company colliery, Lethbridge, *c.* 1904

3

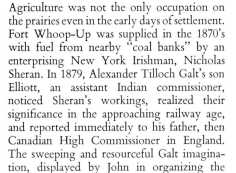

4

5

Agriculture was not the only occupation on the prairies even in the early days of settlement. Fort Whoop-Up was supplied in the 1870's with fuel from nearby "coal banks" by an enterprising New York Irishman, Nicholas Sheran. In 1879, Alexander Tilloch Galt's son Elliott, an assistant Indian commissioner, noticed Sheran's workings, realized their significance in the approaching railway age, and reported immediately to his father, then Canadian High Commissioner in England. The sweeping and resourceful Galt imagination, displayed by John in organizing the Canada Company and by Alexander in opening the Eastern Townships, focused once again in the persons of Alexander and Elliott on an area of Canada soon to be ripe for development.

British capital was secured for a Northwestern Coal and Navigation Company, Lethbridge was founded opposite Sheran's "coal banks" and steamboats were built to take the coal down the Belly River to Medicine Hat, the nearest point on the Canadian Pacific Railway. When river navigation proved unsatisfactory, a narrow-gauge railway was built instead. To exploit land grants received in connection with the railway building, the Alberta Irrigation Company was formed and undertook extensive irrigation projects in conjunction with Mormons immigrating from Utah. One of the Mormons, Jesse Knight, was encouraged to draw on his Utah experience and build Canada's first sugar-beet factory at Raymond to process beets grown on the irrigated land.

Except in the southwestern region where the Galts and the Canadian Pacific Railway were undertaking quite extensive developments depending on coal and irrigation, prairie industry during the early period was confined mainly to some processing of agricultural

6

7

8

products and to improvement in the means of transporting these to the markets of the world. Among the processers, the Calgary cattle king, Pat Burns, built up one of the world's largest meat-packing businesses with branches as far distant as London, Liverpool, and Yokohama. A major role in prairie transportation was played by William Mackenzie and Donald Mann who entered into a partnership in 1896 and pieced together by 1915 a second transcontinental system, the Canadian Northern Railway. On the verge of bankruptcy then, the Canadian Northern had to be taken over by the federal government in 1917, becoming

part of what was organized as the Canadian National Railways system. Another transcontinental attempt at the same time by the Grand Trunk Railway in association with the federal government — the building of the Grand Trunk Pacific as the western section and of the National Transcontinental as the eastern—met a similar fate.

In the midst of these events and commenting on them with raw frontier wit was Canada's most extraordinary journalist, Bob Edwards.

1

41. BRITISH COLUMBIA.
     I, LUMBERING AND FISHING

1. Felling a Douglas fir
2. Hauling logs with team of oxen
3. Salmon fleet awaiting the starting signal
    at Steveston, *c.* 1905

In 1871, when the gold rushes were over, the population of British Columbia had sunk to a mere 10,500, exclusive of the Indians. Growth was very slow during the next decade but with the building of the Canadian Pacific Railway a boom began. By 1911, when the census revealed a population of some 400,000, new railways were being built and the fishing, forest, and mining industries had all advanced well beyond the pioneer stage and were attracting substantial capital investment from Eastern Canada, the United States, Britain, and even Europe. The boom ended, as it did throughout the West, just before the First World War and recovery would not begin until the 1920's.

Some sawmills had been built in the 1840's and in the 1850's but it was not until the 1870's that the lumbermen began their invasion of the stands of huge trees around Burrard Inlet and the erection of steam sawmills to cut lumber for shipment down the coast to San Francisco and South America and across the Pacific to Australia and China. By the 1890's not only had these coastal operations grown to major importance but inland in the Kootenays a valuable lumbering area close to the expanding prairie market was being opened up largely by American capitalists from St. Paul. Another landmark was reached in 1910 when M. J. Scanlon of Minneapolis, encouraged by the previous year's reduction of the American tariff on newsprint, began building the largest

2

3

pulp and paper mill in the West at Powell River.

The fisheries were expanding rapidly as well, particularly the Fraser River salmon fishery centring on Steveston—this latter at a rate depending not only on how many fish could be caught, but on how many could be canned and sold. In big years, when the salmon run was strong the locally built "Columbia River" boats propelled by oar and sail, could easily catch large quantities. To avoid waste and insure fairness to all, canneries would then set boat limits corresponding to their daily capacity and signal the beginning and ending of authorized periods of fishing by the booming of cannon.

The first cannery was in operation in 1870. By the time of the great sockeye run of 1901, total capacity had reached 1,200,000 cases and an inflow of capital was taking place that would speedily consolidate control in the hands of a few large companies.

1

2

3

41. BRITISH COLUMBIA.

II, MINING AND OTHER DEVELOPMENTS

1. Red Mountain, near Rossland
2. Sikh immigrants, c. 1906
3. After the anti-Asiatic riots in Vancouver, 1907
4. War Eagle mine, Rossland
5. The Trail smelter, 1896
6. Beginnings at Prince Rupert, May, 1906
7. Wigwam Inn, c. 1912

The mineral discoveries in the East and West Kootenays in the early 1890's drew attention to British Columbia in a way reminiscent of the Cariboo. There were important differences, of course. More than one mineral was involved —silver, lead, zinc, and copper in addition to gold—and, instead of simple placer mining, heavy capital expenditure was required to open mine shafts and undertake the research and provide the equipment needed to separate the metals from the rock in which they were embedded and from one another. A few figures showing British Columbia's production of the key minerals in 1891 as compared with 1901 illustrate the rapidity with which wealth was nevertheless extracted from the Silver King mine at Nelson and the great Sullivan mine at Kimberley, from Red Mountain with its War Eagle, Centre Star, Le Roi, and other mines at Rossland, and from the silver-lead-zinc ledges at Slocan. Gold production rose from $400,000 in 1891 to $5,320,000 in 1901; silver from $3300 to $3,306,000; and lead and copper from zero to $2,235,000 and $4,500,000 respectively.

The first smelter at Trail, linked by narrow-gauge railway with the mines at Rossland, was completed in 1896 by "Fritz" Heinze

4

5

6

7

of Butte, Montana. Heinze's and other American investments at this time point to the fact that the initial opening of the Kootenays represented essentially a turning northward of the American mining frontier. Before connections across the border could be consolidated, however, action was taken by the Canadian Pacific Railway. Alert to the region and familiar with the rich coal deposits in the East Kootenays it negotiated the Crow's Nest Pass Agreement with the federal government obtaining land and mineral subsidies, built its Crow's Nest Pass branch line which would eventually be extended to the coast,

and bought out Heinze's smelter and railway holdings. In 1906 along with Rossland mining interests, it participated in the formation of the Consolidated Mining and Smelting Company.

The booming progress in mining, lumbering, and fishing in the 1900's was supplemented by a new surge of railway building, particularly the Canadian Northern's advance down the Thompson and Fraser towards Vancouver and the Grand Trunk Pacific's towards Prince Rupert in an attempt to make it a great Pacific terminus. Optimism and prosperity, symbolized by the Wigwam Inn and many other examples of fashionable living,

had become the rule. The only jarring note was labour trouble accentuated by the growing anti-Asiatic feeling. Imported from the early days of mining and railway building as cheap contract labour and flowing in as well in increasing numbers to escape over-crowding at home, Chinese, Japanese, and East Indians had become feared competitors of the white working class. Troubles flared from time to time culminating in riots in Vancouver in 1907 and the burning and looting of Nanaimo in 1913.

1

2

3

4

5   6

In marked contrast to the booming western provinces, the Maritimes and Newfoundland pursued their traditional ways with little change in their economies and little growth of population. Their basic industries, conducted in much the same way as they had always been, were still fishing, farming, lumbering, and shipbuilding, with the latter less prosperous in the developing age of steam and steel than it had been in the great days of sail. The coal of Nova Scotia remained important and in 1895 mining of the huge iron ore deposits on Bell Island, Newfoundland, began. A large market for both was opened up when the great blast furnaces at Sydney, Nova Scotia, came into production in 1901 and began turning out a major proportion of Canada's pig iron and steel.

Although the Atlantic region was not in general experiencing the rapid changes characteristic of the rest of Canada, it continued its boasted export of brains and witnessed experiments in connection with two of the most significant advances of the twentieth century. The first occurred in December 1901, when Marconi received in the Cabot Tower at St. John's, Newfoundland, the first trans-

7

8

9

10

Atlantic wireless signal from a station he had built in Cornwall, England. Less fleetingly linked with Canada was the work of Alexander Graham Bell. Having already become famous through his invention of the telephone, Bell founded at Baddeck, Nova Scotia, in 1907 an Aerial Experiment Association. As a result of its efforts, one of its members, J. A. D. McCurdy, made in 1909 in his *Silver Dart* the first aeroplane flight in the British Empire. Bell spent most of his later life at Baddeck continuing to experiment with planes and also with hydrofoils and he was buried there in 1922.

Fire that might devastate a large area was a hazard common to most Canadian towns and cities where water supplies, fire-fighting equipment, and fire-prevention regulations were all as a rule inadequate. The fire that struck St. John's, Newfoundland, so disastrously on July 8, 1892, was therefore by no means unique: it destroyed 1700 buildings, left 11,000 homeless, and caused $13,000,000 property damage.

43. ONTARIO AND QUEBEC.
I, LUMBERING ON THE OTTAWA

1. Broad axe
2. Log branding iron
3. Lumbermen's shanty, 1871
4. Sawmill with circular saws, 1872
5. J. R. Booth timber raft
6. A raft in the Lachine rapids

Lumbering was one of the great industries of the St. Lawrence and Great Lakes region throughout the nineteenth century. In the lowlands near the St. Lawrence and north of the lower Lakes, it gave way to agriculture as the forests were cleared. Up the Ottawa and the more easterly tributaries of the St. Lawrence leading into the rocky Canadian Shield, it remained of primary importance until the depletion of the great stands of white and red pine and changing markets led to its gradual replacement as the century closed by the manufacturing of pulp and paper.

Woods operations remained much the same throughout the century. Men and teams of horses or oxen went into the cutting area in the fall—having to go farther upstream each year as the virgin stands receded. Crude log shanties were built, their walls lined with bunks, and openings left in the roofs through which smoke from the built-up hearth fireplaces in the centre could escape. Stacked around were hay and bags of oats for the animals and barrels of pork, flour, beans, corn syrup, tea, soap, and tobacco for the men.

All winter trees were cut and were roughly —and wastefully—squared with broad axes, given ownership brands, and hauled to the streams down which they were floated in the spring. At convenient collection points, they were fastened together into 24-foot wide cribs, a number of which in turn were joined to make huge rafts—rafts that could be easily

4

5

6

broken up again into individual cribs to run rapids or slides.

Hull first and then Bytown (Ottawa after 1855) began as lumbering centres opposite one another at the foot of the great Chaudière Falls of the Ottawa River. Philemon Wright, the founder of Hull, floated the first timber raft down to Quebec City in 1806 and in 1817 built the Ottawa River's first steamboat. His son Ruggles, copying what he had seen in Scandinavia, built Canada's first timber slide in 1829 to by-pass the Chaudière Falls, making it 26 feet wide to accommodate a complete crib. Thousands of cribs a year were soon running this slide and riding them became for

distinguished visitors such as the Prince of Wales in 1860 as essential to a tour of Canada as being photographed at Niagara Falls.

By the 1870's when the square timber trade was reaching its peak and the production of sawn lumber was continuing to increase rapidly, the Hull-Ottawa region had become a major centre for both, owing to its natural advantages and also to the ability and capital investment of a few men who had arrived twenty years before and had since made fortunes themselves. F. H. Bronson, a New York lumberman, had come in 1852 and built the first large mill for the export trade in sawn lumber to the United States, a trade that

boomed with the signing of the Reciprocity Treaty in 1854. In 1854 E. B. Eddy, also from the United States, began making matches by hand in Hull, founding what would become an enormous enterprise. J. R. Booth, from Quebec's Eastern Townships, began with a small shingle factory in Hull in 1857, secured the contract for the timber of the new Parliament Building in Ottawa shortly afterwards, and went on to a variety of large-scale forest operations including eventually the manufacturing of pulp and paper.

43. ONTARIO AND QUEBEC.
     II, THE SQUARE TIMBER TRADE

1. Cookery on J. R. Booth raft
2. Cook shanty on raft
3. Loading timber, 1872
4. The timber coves at Quebec, 1872

The value of Canada's trade in square timber was considerably less even at its peak in the 1870's than that in sawn lumber, but from the time of Philemon Wright's first raft in 1806 until J. R. Booth's last in 1904, it created a way of life on the Ottawa River as distinctive as that of the voyageurs of fur-trading days and one that was not dissimilar; indeed many of the Nile "voyageurs" of 1884 were in every-day life Ottawa raftsmen.

After a winter in the woods rafting crews, averaging a man a crib, spent the summer on rafts, working the oars and the heavy 24-foot sweeps with which they were guided down stream, sleeping in the small huts and gathering about the cookeries for meals, breaking up the rafts and taking individual cribs down slides or rapids, walking back again for other cribs until all were through, re-rafting the cribs, and having eventually reached the timber coves, going on a spree at Quebec before starting back up-river again.

The trade in square timber depended almost exclusively on the British market. It had begun when Napoleon's Continental System had in 1808 cut Britain off from Baltic supplies and the development of alternative sources within the British Empire had been urgently undertaken by means of tariff preferences and other forms of encouragement. The preferences had been reduced in the 1820's and on several subsequent occasions but were not

3

4

finally abolished until 1860. By that time Canadian square timber was in any case fully competitive and hundreds of ships a year were being loaded at Quebec and others at Saint John, New Brunswick, as well. Exports continued to climb, reaching their peak value of $7,322,000 in 1877 when they made up over one-tenth of Canada's export total.

43. ONTARIO AND QUEBEC.
III, OIL AND ELECTRICITY

1. Abraham Gesner
2. Oil wells at Petrolia
3. Atlantic Petroleum Works, London, c. 1870
4. Crude oil stills, Imperial Oil's Petrolia refinery, 1893
5. Sir Adam Beck
6. Shawinigan Water and Power Company, c. 1904
7. Shawinigan, with second power plant added
8. Early automobile

Kerosene was first extracted from coal and petroleum by a Nova Scotian, Abraham Gesner, who obtained a patent and began production in the United States in 1854. Its popularity for use in lamps and stoves encouraged petroleum production in both Canada and the United States. James Williams sunk the first well at Oil Springs, Canada West, in 1857, Edwin Drake the first at Titusville, Pennsylvania, in 1859 and others followed shortly in both regions. In Canada where the centre shifted seven miles north to Petrolia, annual production by 1863 was

already 100,000 barrels and by 1895 it had reached a high of 800,000.

From the early 1860's until 1885, refining was concentrated mainly in London where plants were built by the Spencers, the Watermans, the Hodgens, Jacob Englehart, Thomas H. Smallman, and a number of others. Smallman founded as well a company for manufacturing the sulphuric acid needed in the refining process.

Markets expanded rapidly but production in both Ontario and Pennsylvania more than kept pace. By 1880 when prices had fallen

from one dollar a gallon to twelve cents a number of prominent London producers decided on amalgamation and formed the Imperial Oil Company. In 1885 the Company's headquarters and main refining operations were transferred to Petrolia and in 1899 to Sarnia where the crude oil from Petrolia could be brought in by pipe line and additional supplies could be imported by barge from Ohio. By this time, the whole industry was on the verge of the revolutionary change that would come with the introduction of the automobile.

5

6

7

8

Electricity had been coming into increasing use meanwhile, ever since Edison's invention of the incandescent bulb in 1879, for domestic and street lighting. By the end of the century street railway companies and certain types of manufacturing plants were also employing it extensively. The introduction of high-tension transmission techniques at about this time made hydro-electric installations at relatively distant sites feasible—a development of great importance for Quebec and Ontario, both of which had huge water power resources but lacked coal for more conveniently located thermal electric plants. By 1900, Canada's installed hydro-electric capacity was 173,000 h.p. The completion by Shawinigan Water and Power Company of its first two 5000 h.p. units on the St. Maurice River in 1903 was only one of a number of rapid steps forward—notable at the time although dwarfed by later developments—that brought the total to 177,000 by 1910.

Of unique importance in Ontario was the setting up as early as 1906 of the Hydro-Electric Power Commission of Ontario. Largely the creation of Adam Beck, its first chairman, it arose out of an enquiry into the possibility of obtaining cheap power from the Niagara River that had been initiated in 1903 by a group of municipalities from Toronto westward, including London where Beck was mayor and a member of the provincial legislature. The commission began by purchasing power and building transmission lines to thirteen municipalities in Western Ontario. Later it would generate power as well and extend its activities to all parts of the province.

43. ONTARIO AND QUEBEC.
    IV, PULP AND PAPER AND MINING

1. Interior of the Laurentides Pulp Mill, Grand'Mère
2. Its exterior, *c.* 1896
3. The same, *c.* 1901
4. LaRose Mine, Cobalt, *c.* 1910
5. Crown Chartered Mine, Porcupine, *c.* 1910
6. Asbestos mine, Beaver Pit, Eastern Townships, *c.* 1904

Two increasingly heavy users of hydro-electric power in the first decade of the twentieth century were the mining and pulp and paper industries.

Paper, made from rags in Canada since early in the nineteenth century, was first made from wood pulp when a mill for grinding pulp was built in 1866 at Valleyfield, Quebec, followed by one for making pulp by a chemical process at Windsor Mills, Quebec, in 1869. Others were built as the century went on and output increased substantially. Quebec retained its initial lead, the St. Maurice basin playing a major role in this because of its huge stands of spruce and balsam and its falls already being harnessed at Shawinigan and Grand'Mère to supply the enormous power requirements of the mills.

Legislation in both Canada and the United States stimulated the upsurge in production that took place shortly after the twentieth century began. In Canada where there was growing concern over the very large amount of pulpwood being exported for use in American mills, Ontario first and then other provinces placed an embargo on that cut on crown lands, a considerable part of the total. In the United States, a lowering of the tariff on newsprint begun in 1909 was followed by total abolition shortly afterwards. With its pulpwood resources secure and the door open to the great and rapidly growing American market, Canada was set to become the world's major producer of newsprint.

Mining began in Northern Ontario in the last decades of the nineteenth century, as it had earlier in the huge asbestos region of the Eastern Townships, as a result of discoveries made during railway construction. The first

5

6

find, when the Canadian Pacific Railway was being put through in 1883, was the great copper-nickel basin around Sudbury. Valued initially for its copper, it proved even more important for its nickel when a market for that metal was created by proving to the British and French governments that nickel steel was far superior to the ordinary kind for warship armour and other military purposes. By 1914, large smelters and power plants had been built and production was in full swing with 22,758 tons of nickel and 14,474 of copper being extracted.

It was the building of the Temiskaming and Northern Ontario Railway, intended to give access to the agricultural clay belt of Northern Ontario, that led to the discovery by Fred LaRose in 1903 of a rich vein of silver mixed with cobalt at what became Cobalt. A syndicate in which the leading figure was Noah Timmins bought LaRose's and various other claims and began such successful mining operations that in 1906 and 1907 a boom took place reminiscent of the Klondike—and with some of the same men participating. Similarly rich discoveries of gold at Porcupine in 1909

attracted Cobalt and other capital, particularly that of Noah Timmins. By 1912, the town of Timmins was incorporated after having been linked to the outside by railway, and the rich Hollinger, Dome, and McIntyre mines were already becoming famous. In January of that same year, in the vicinity of Kirkland Lake where gold had been discovered in 1906, Harry Oakes and others staked claims to what became at the height of its production Canada's greatest gold mine. Meanwhile across the border in Quebec, other rich mineral deposits still awaited the prospector.

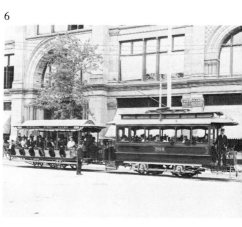

43. ONTARIO AND QUEBEC.
     V, MONTREAL

1. The harbour, c. 1878
2. Ice shove in the harbour, c. 1884
3. The ice palace, 1885
4. St. James Cathedral, c. 1909
5. Sherbrooke St., c. 1897
6. Electric streetcars on St. Catherine St., 1895
7. Teeing off at the Mount Royal, c. 1909
8. "Hockey Match, Victoria Rink," 1893

In a central Canada undergoing substantial urban and industrial growth, Montreal and Toronto began to take on a metropolitan character as the nineteeth century drew to a close. Their populations which had been 155,000 and 96,000 respectively in 1881 were, by 1901, 328,000 and 210,000. By 1911 they were 491,000 and 382,000.

Montreal's strategic location at the head of navigation at the entrance to one of the great inland waterways of the world had been the basic reason for its importance from the days of the fur trade. Railway and canal building had added to the city's advantages and the opening of the West, served by the Canadian Pacific Railway of which it was the eastern terminus, made it by 1900 the major focal point of Canadian trade and finance. Its harbour with the long granite wall and sloping ramps built in the 1840's was continuously busy with shipping—except of course in winter, Montreal's greatest economic handicap. Sherbrooke Street became lined with the fine sandstone houses of the wealthy. Nearby a new St. James Cathedral rose as Bishop Bourget's reminder—underlined by his copying of St. Peter's in Rome—that, despite the prosperity brought by English

3

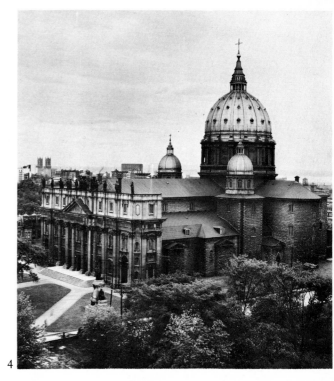

4

7

8

business, Montreal was still in the majority French and Roman Catholic.

Many of Montreal's problems were common to all growing North American cities and were solved in the usual ways. In the 1840's and 1850's a municipal water system and gas lighting were provided. A street railway with horse-drawn vehicles began operating in 1864. Telephones came in the 1880's along with electricity for street and domestic lighting. By 1894, the street railway also was fully electrified and was able to offer more rapid service making feasible the extension of lines and the opening up of more distant suburbs.

Sports became more fully organized especially after the formation of the Montreal Amateur Athletic Association in 1884. Curling, snowshoeing, and after 1874 bicycling were all popular as were golf, cricket, lacrosse, and football. Hockey, played after 1875 according to the McGill Rules, was already becoming a spectator sport. A feature of the 1880's was the annual winter carnival which always had as its climax the storming of the great ice palace.

121

Toronto was like Montreal only in the ways in which all expanding nineteenth century American cities were similar. It went through the various stages of acquiring water and sewers, street lighting, a street railway, and other public services. It spread out geographically: the coming of age of Toronto has been associated with its annexation of Yorkville in 1883 and of thirteen other neighbouring communities in the following ten years. In the 1890's it built a massive new City Hall designed by a local architect, Edward J. Lennox, in the modern American version of Romanesque, the "progressive" style of the age. Various sports and amusements were popular as they were in Montreal, but Torontonians could take special pride when they visited Hanlan's Point in thinking of Ned Hanlan who had been brought up there and had in 1881 won for Canada its first world championship in a famous race against an Australian oarsman on the English Thames.

By the end of the century Toronto and Montreal were rivals in trade and finance, but they were widely divergent from one another in several vital respects. Most obvious was the striking contrast between Toronto's highly homogeneous British Protestant population and Montreal's division between a French Roman Catholic majority and a powerful

4

5

6

English Protestant minority. Equally fundamental, however, were the differences in their economies.

Toronto lacked the advantage that Montreal had had from fur-trading days of being the focal point of a widespread continental and trans-Atlantic system. It had on the other hand, to a far greater extent than Montreal, an immediate and expanding economic hinterland of rich farms, prosperous towns, growing cities, and, on the northern fringes, lumbering and a developing mining industry. The experience and the financial and manufacturing facilities acquired in the service of this original Ontario hinterland provided Toronto with the

opportunity—readily seized—of extending its economic influence further westward on much the same basis when the main routes to the West were tapped by railways to several ports on Lake Huron and Georgian Bay and to the main Canadian Pacific Railway line at Nipissing.

With differences in their economies such as these, Montreal tended to have a ranging cosmopolitan outlook while Toronto remained essentially a country town grown large. Characteristic was Toronto's delight in its agricultural fairs which became annual events in the form of Toronto Industrial Exhibition in 1879 and took the title Canadian

National Exhibition in 1912. The departmental stores of Timothy Eaton and Robert Simpson, founded in 1869 and 1872 respectively, were similarly urban and more sophisticated versions of country general stores such as Eaton had helped run for many years at St. Marys. It is not without significance that Eaton had the imagination to appeal to his old customers by issuing his first catalogue in 1884 to out-of-town visitors to the Exhibition— and that they responded with an enthusiasm that added a new and typically Torontonian dimension to his business.

1

44. THE NORTH.

I, TRAILS TO THE KLONDIKE

1. Below the White Pass
2. Building boats on Lake Lindemann
3. Ascending the Chilkoot Pass
4. Packers on the Chilkoot
5. The Canadian boundary line at the top of Chilkoot Pass

When news reached the outside world in July 1897 that rich gold discoveries had been made the previous August in the Klondike region of the Canadian Yukon the last great gold rush in North America began. "Klondikitis," as the newspapers called it, spread like a disease through North America and far beyond, even infecting a group of New Zealand Maoris. Thousands of men and a considerable number of women from around the world and from all walks of life started immediately to converge by a variety of routes on the junction of the Klondike and Yukon rivers where Dawson City rose suddenly from the wooded hillside

and within a year had a population of 25,000.

The majority approached by ship up the Pacific coast and into the Lynn Canal landing at Skagway or Dyea. From Skagway a trail crossed the White Pass to Lake Bennett—but of some 5000 who attempted it in the fall of 1897 only a handful reached Dawson before winter. The higher and steeper Chilkoot Pass from Dyea to Lake Lindemann had the advantage of being more direct and was the more popular during that winter, when an incredible 22,000 persons were checked through the boundary station at its summit by the North West Mounted Police.

And it was not simply a matter of each man (or sometimes woman) taking his place once in the four-mile long line climbing in the "Chilkoot Lockstep" from Sheep's Camp to the summit. Each was required by police regulations to bring with him a year's supply of food which meant, along with tents, clothing, and equipment, about a ton of goods in all. Weary shuttling between caches became necessary; men carried 65-pound packs upward and slid swiftly down again in one of the grooves worn beside the trail. For those who could afford it, there was by the spring of 1898 an ingenious aerial tramway—fourteen

2

3   4

5

miles of copper-steel cable supported by huge tripods with steam engines at each end—capable of moving goods forward in 300-pound carloads at a rate of one a minute.

All through winter the lines moved upward across the passes to the adjoining Lakes Bennett and Lindemann. By spring the shores of both were lined with tents and the saws and hammers were busy from dawn till dusk preparing lumber and building over 7000 boats for the 500-mile voyage that still remained down the Lewes and Yukon rivers to Dawson.

44. THE NORTH. II, DAWSON CITY

1. Snake-hips Lulu
2. Victorian Order nurses and Toronto *Globe* reporter, Faith Fenton (seated, right)
3. Palace Grand theatre and dance hall, Dawson City
4. Street scene, Whitehorse, May, 1901
5. Pine Creek and City
6. Street scene, Dawson City
7. Canadian Bank of Commerce party en route to Dawson City, June, 1898
8. Gold shipment ($750,000) from Canadian Bank of Commerce, Dawson City, Sept. 20, 1899
9. Underground at Eldorado

The arrival of the boats at Dawson in June 1898, transformed it immediately into a bustling gold-rush town with streets of tents and shacks, saloons and churches, stores, barber shops, newspaper offices and, as early as July 1, two banks. The Bank of British North America and the Canadian Bank of Commerce had both dispatched parties across the passes and down river with the leading flotillas. The Bank of British North America was the first to set up for business—in a tent—but the Commerce having had the foresight to bring in gold-assaying equipment was the first to begin buying gold dust and shipping it out.

During the next year or so life in Dawson began to take on a regular if not necessarily an orderly tempo. The mine workings proved as rich as had been hoped for. In 1900, when gold production was at its height, it amounted to 1,350,000 fine ounces valued at $22,250,000. Over an eight-year period from 1897 it totalled $100,000,000.

Much of this wealth, won laboriously from the hillsides and streams, slipped easily through the fingers of the miners in the saloons and dance halls of Dawson, notably the Palace Grand built and opulently furnished during the winter of 1898-99 by "Arizona

5

7

6

8

9

Charlie" Meadows, formerly with "Buffalo Bill" Cody's Wild West Show.

Not all of the women in Dawson belonged to the dance-halls, although those that did are usually thought of first. There were hard-working wives as well, some of whom had helped their husbands pack supplies across the passes. There was Belinda Mulrony, the tough shrewd proprietor of the richly appointed Fairview Hotel, and there was Faith Benton, a Toronto *Globe* reporter. One summer there were two wealthy tourists, one an admiral's daughter, the other the niece of a former United States president. As unexpected as any were four Victorian Order nurses, there because the governor general's wife, the energetic Lady Aberdeen, having won her battle against the prejudices of the medical profession and organized the public-health nursing service in 1897, was ready to seize the opportunity of sending some of its first members—under carefully arranged North West Mounted Police protection—into an area where they could do much good and at the same time receive much favourable publicity.

1

44. THE NORTH. III, CONTINUING EXPLORATION

1. Sir Edward Belcher's sailing ship *Assistance* being towed by steam tender *Pioneer*, c. 1852

2. A. P. Low's *Neptune* in winter quarters at Cape Fullerton, Hudson Bay, 1903-04

3. York boats

4. Tracking on the Athabaska River, c. 1901. C. W. Mathers photograph

5. Hudson's Bay Company freight schedules on the Athabaska

6. Red River carts portaging fur at Fort Smith, c. 1903

3

Except in the Klondike, life in the Canadian North continued with little change over the generations. Trade remained largely in the hands of the Hudson's Bay Company and was conducted in the traditional manner using the familiar York boats and Red River carts. British explorers like Belcher, Hall, and Nares continued the work begun by Ross and Franklin, laying a firm foundation for Britain's claim to the Arctic Islands—a claim transferred voluntarily to Canada on September 1, 1880.

The Canadian government, preoccupied with the opening of the West, was little interested in the North for some time although in the 1890's it did sponsor important overland journeys by J. B. Tyrrell and in the early twentieth century coastal explorations by A. P. Low, J. E. Bernier, and Vilhjalmur Stefansson. The most spectacular accomplishments of this period, however, were those of the Norwegian, Roald Amundsen, who finally succeeded in the old objective of navigating a northwest Passage (1903-06), and of the American, Robert E. Peary, who reached the North Pole in 1909.

2

5

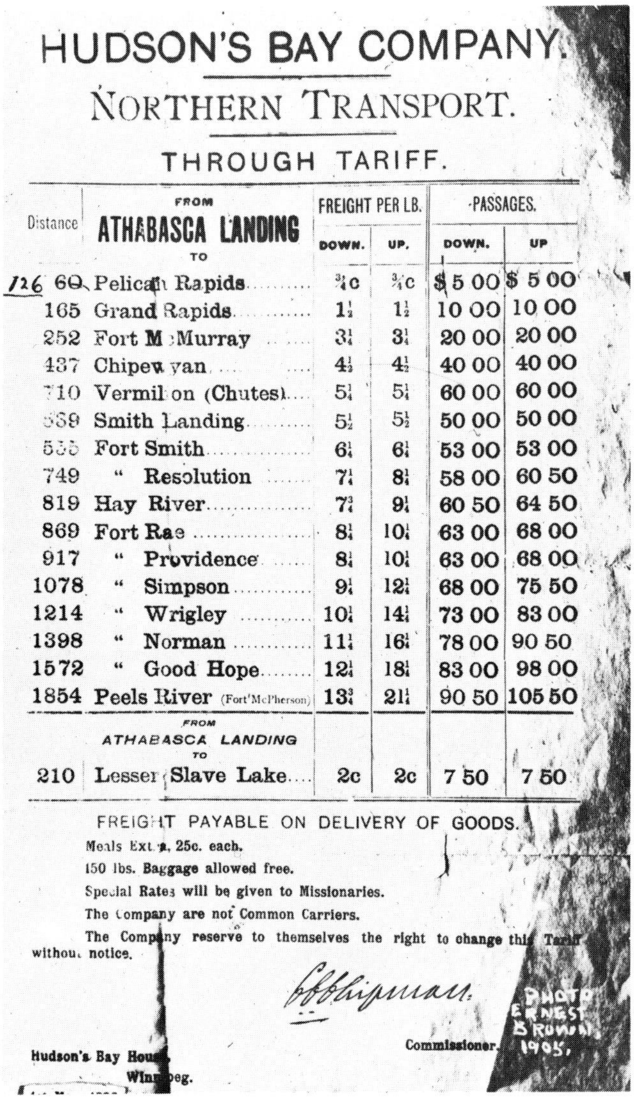

HUDSON'S BAY COMPANY.

NORTHERN TRANSPORT.

THROUGH TARIFF.

Distance	FROM ATHABASCA LANDING TO	FREIGHT PER LB. DOWN.	FREIGHT PER LB. UP.	PASSAGES. DOWN.	PASSAGES. UP
126 60	Pelican Rapids	¾c	¾c	$ 5 00	$ 5 00
165	Grand Rapids	1½	1½	10 00	10 00
252	Fort McMurray	3¼	3¼	20 00	20 00
437	Chipewyan	4½	4½	40 00	40 00
710	Vermilion (Chutes)	5¼	5¼	60 00	60 00
559	Smith Landing	5½	5½	50 00	50 00
555	Fort Smith	6¼	6¼	53 00	53 00
749	" Resolution	7¼	8¼	58 00	60 50
819	Hay River	7¾	9¼	60 50	64 50
869	Fort Rae	8¼	10¼	63 00	68 00
917	" Providence	8¼	10¼	63 00	68 00
1078	" Simpson	9¼	12¼	68 00	75 50
1214	" Wrigley	10¼	14¼	73 00	83 00
1398	" Norman	11¼	16¼	78 00	90 50
1572	" Good Hope	12¼	18¼	83 00	98 00
1854	Peels River (Fort McPherson)	13¾	21¼	90 50	105 50
	FROM ATHABASCA LANDING TO				
210	Lesser Slave Lake	2c	2c	7 50	7 50

FREIGHT PAYABLE ON DELIVERY OF GOODS.

Meals Extra, 25c. each.

150 lbs. Baggage allowed free.

Special Rates will be given to Missionaries.

The Company are not Common Carriers.

The Company reserve to themselves the right to change this Tariff without notice.

C.C. Chipman

Commissioner.

Hudson's Bay House,
Winnipeg.

4

6

1

2

3

7

10 11

45 POLITICAL TENSIONS

1. John A. Macdonald in old age
2. Oliver Mowat
3. Honoré Mercier
4. W. S. Fielding
5. Bishop Ignace Bourget
6. D'Alton McCarthy
7. Macdonald's funeral procession leaving Parliament Hill, June 10, 1891
8. Conference of Provincial Premiers at Quebec, Oct. 20, 1887. Seated left to right, A. G. Blair (N.B.), Honoré Mercier (Que.) Oliver Mowat (Ont.), W. S. Fielding (N.S.), John Norquay (Man.)
9. Saskatchewan inaugural ceremonies. Sept. 4, 1905. Seated: left, Laurier, centre, Earl Grey
10. Edward Blake
11. J. J. C. Abbott
12. John Thompson
13. Mackenzie Bowell
14. Charles Tupper

The decline of the Conservative party and increasing friction between English and French Canada, together with a rising emphasis on provincial rights generally, made the last decades of the nineteenth century and the first of the twentieth a time of severe political tension. Even Macdonald with all his political skill found it more and more difficult to keep country — and his party — together. The problem was less with the official opposition in Ottawa led by the coldly intellectual Edward Blake and after 1887 by the still untried Wilfrid Laurier, than with the provincial premiers —

5

6

8

9

12

13

14

Oliver Mowat, the long-time and shrewd proponent of provincial rights in Ontario; Honoré Mercier, the ambitious Quebec nationalist; W. S. Fielding, willing to threaten repeal of the union to get better terms for Nova Scotia; and even Conservative John Norquay of Manitoba, opposed as his whole province was to the Macdonald-supported Canadian Pacific Railway monopoly. The conference of provincial premiers called by Mercier in 1887 seemed a culmination of the danger but actually made little stir in the face of Macdonald's bland indifference.

More serious was the widening gulf between extreme Roman Catholic opinion in Quebec as exemplified by Bishop Bourget of Montreal and the equally extreme and intolerant views of D'Alton McCarthy and the Equal Rights Association of Ontario. School questions in New Brunswick, Ontario, Manitoba, and the Northwest, this latter at the time Saskatchewan and Alberta were being made provinces in 1905, provoked particularly violent disagreement and became serious threats to national unity. The death of Macdonald and the rapid succession of Abbott, Thompson,

Bowell, and Tupper to the prime-ministership weakened the federal government as well as the Conservative party and not only prepared the way for Laurier's victory in 1896 but bequeathed him problems of unusual importance and difficulty.

46. CANADA AND THE EMPIRE

1. Nile "voyageurs" on Parliament Hill, 1884

2. Sir Wilfrid Laurier

3. The premiers at Hawarden during the Colonial Conference of 1897. Left to right: Louis Davies, Wilfrid Laurier, W. E. Gladstone, Mr. Reed (Australia), Mr. Seddon (New Zealand)

4. Troops aboard S.S. *Monterey* chartered by Lord Strathcona

5. Gordon Highlanders and Royal Canadian Regiment crossing Paardeberg Drift,

Feb. 18, 1900

6. After the Battle of Paardeberg, Feb. 19, 1900

7. Henri Bourassa

8. Laurier at Sorel, 1911

9. Robert Borden and Winston Churchill leaving Admiralty, 1912

10. H.M.C.S. *Niobe*

11. Coaling the *Niobe*, Halifax Dockyard, *c.* 1914

The wave of jingoistic imperialism that swept Western Europe and North America as the nineteenth century drew to a close caught up many English-speaking Canadians, especially recent arrivals from the British Isles. Most French Canadians, led by Henri Bourassa, rejected it. Laurier, recognizing his responsibility as prime minister to both groups, tried to pursue a moderate course not unlike that of Macdonald before him.

At the first Colonial Conference in 1897, amid the enthusiasm of Queen Victoria's Diamond Jubilee celebrations, Laurier firmly resisted moves in the direction of Imperial Federation. When the South African War broke out he tried to follow the example set by Macdonald in 1884 during Britain's troubles in the Sudan. Macdonald had permitted the

7

8

9

10

11

enlistment of almost 400 Canadian boatmen, who had played a valuable role in Wolseley's Nile expedition, but had refused official military assistance. In the more serious circumstances of the South African War, Laurier went so far as to authorize the sending of two volunteer militia expeditions and the raising of other troops in Canada by the British government and by Lord Strathcona. In all some 7300 Canadians served in South Africa, distinguishing themselves on a number of occasions including the Battle of Paardeberg.

The South African War was hardly over when the Canadian Government came under heavy pressure from Britain and from within

Canada to assist in meeting the German Navy's growing challenge to British supremacy at sea. Canadian opinion became deeply divided. Bourassa, at one extreme, believed no naval expenditure was justified; Robert Borden, the new Conservative leader, and many others favoured direct and substantial assistance to the Royal Navy. Laurier steered a middle course in his Naval Service Act of 1910 creating an independent Canadian Navy. Its first ships, purchased that same year, were two old British cruisers, the *Niobe* and the *Rainbow*. When Borden became prime minister and was convinced by Churchill of the seriousness of the German threat, he tried unsuccessfully to

reverse Laurier's policy and provide direct aid on an emergency basis to the Royal Navy. The debate was long and bitter and little was accomplished one way or the other before the First World War began.

2

6

1

3

47. THE FIRST WORLD WAR. I, IN CANADA

1. The first contingent from Youngstown, Alberta
2. Volunteers from the Klondike
3. Raw recruits at Valcartier
4. Princess Patricia inspecting Canadian troops
5. Departure for overseas
6. Submarines built at Vickers, Montreal
7. Laurier addressing Montreal crowd urging voluntary enlistment, Sept. 28, 1916
8. Burning of Parliament Buildings, Feb. 3, 1916
9. War work for women
10. Results of explosion of French ship *Mont Blanc* in Halifax harbour, Dec. 6, 1917

9

Canada along with the whole British Empire was automatically included in Britain's declaration of war on Germany on August 4, 1914. A tremendous outburst of patriotic enthusiasm followed. Volunteers for a Canadian Expeditionary Force began pouring in from far and near to a mobilization camp hastily created at Valcartier, Quebec. Ex-British regulars and Canadian veterans of the South African War were formed into a special battalion, the Princess Patricia Canadian Light Infantry, named in honour of the popular daughter of of the Governor General, the Duke of Connaught. The rest were given what training and

equipment was possible. By October 3, ten British warships were escorting thirty-two transports carrying 33,000 men out into the Gulf of St. Lawrence en route to England. On January 4, 1915, exactly five months after the declaration of war, the first Canadians, the Princess Pats, entered the front lines in France.

It was a remarkable beginning for a country as ill-prepared and lacking in experience as Canada but was characteristic of what was to follow. The manufacturing of war requirements, including even some submarines, became varied and enlarged far beyond expectations and primary production from farm,

forest, mine, and sea was rapidly expanded despite labour shortages.

The manpower problem, critical from almost the beginning, became of central importance as trench warfare with its heavy losses continued. By 1917, with a total population of some 8,060,000 Canada had over 300,000 in its Expeditionary Force and had suffered over 50,000 fatal casualties. Despite energetic recruiting efforts, not least by Laurier who was trying desperately to avoid the alternative of conscription, volunteer enlistments had become insufficient to supply the need for overseas reinforcements.

7

8

5

4

10

47. THE FIRST WORLD WAR. II, IN THE TRENCHES

1. Clearing a trench near Lens, Aug. 1917
2. Shrapnel bursting over trench, 1916
3. Infantry wearing new helmets, April, 1916
4. Front-line sentry, Sept. 1916
5. Smashing barbed wire with mortar, May, 1917
6. Over the top, Oct. 1916
7. Pte. Tom Longboat, Indian long-distance runner, buying newspaper, June, 1917
8. First aid at Courcelette, Sept. 1916

9. Trenches near Passchendaele, 1917
10. Captured Prussian guards aiding wounded Canadians
11. Minister of Militia, Lt-Gen. Sir Sam Hughes (accompanied by Lord Rothermere, in civilian clothes) on the Somme Front, 1916
12. Front-line Y.M.C.A. hut, Aug. 1917
13. The Dumbells

The "front" for the Canadian Expeditionary Force during the long weary months from the spring of 1915 until the great German offensive three years later was a network of muddy trenches stretching from the Channel coast of Belgium through to and beyond the Somme in France punctuated by names that were becoming part of Canadian history—Passchendaele, Ypres, St. Eloi, Festhubert, Givenchy, Lens, Vimy, Arras, and Courcelette. The chaplaincy service, the Y.M.C.A., distinguished visitors, and in the last two years, the Canadian Army Third Division Concert Party, the famous Dumbells, did what could be done to relieve the horror of one of the great bloodbaths of history.

4

5

6

10

11

12

13

47. THE FIRST WORLD WAR. III, VIMY RIDGE

1. Consolidating position on Vimy Ridge, April, 1917
2. Machine gunners digging in, April, 1917
3. Naval gun firing over the Ridge, May, 1917
4. King George V, General Currie, and General Horne on Vimy Ridge, July, 1917
5. Observation balloon descending
6. Vimy Ridge trenches from balloon, Nov. 1917

7. Aerial dog fight
8. German prisoners captured at Vimy, May, 1917
9. His Majesty's Pigeon Service, Nov. 1917
10. Canadians in main street of Vimy, May, 1917
11. Fort Garry Horse on Cambrai front, Dec. 1917
12. Tank crossing German front line at Vimy, Nov. 1917

Although the Battle of Vimy Ridge in April 1917 was only one of many assaults undertaken against the enemy lines during the long years of virtual stalemate on the western front, it has particular significance in Canadian history as the first exclusively Canadian victory.

The Ridge had been occupied and heavily fortified by the Germans since late in 1914 and all previous attempts to dislodge them had failed. As part of a co-ordinated Allied attack at several points along the front, a major assault by all four divisions of the Canadian Corps was decided upon. Preparations in-

cluded several weeks of heavier than usual bombardment and aeroplane flights over the enemy trenches. Action began early on April 9, Easter Sunday morning, with a brief but an extremely intense barrage of artillery and machine gun fire. An infantry advance across No Man's Land followed, overwhelming all resistance. By nightfall most of the ridge was in Canadian hands. After several more days of mopping up the victory had been won—at a cost by no means high for that sort of warfare of 10,602 casualties, 3,598 of them fatal.

1

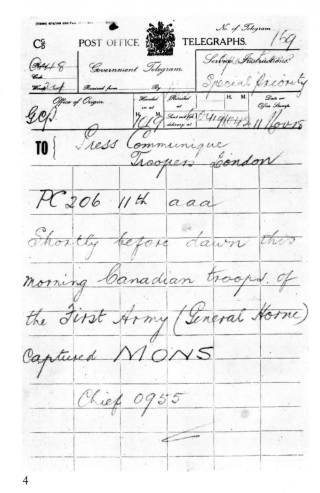

2

3

47. THE FIRST WORLD WAR.
    IV, CONSCRIPTION AND PEACE

1. Election poster in Canadian hospital in England, Dec. 1917
2. Imperial War Conference, 1917
3. Canadians passing through Ypres
4. Mons telegram, Nov. 11, 1918
5. The Peace Conference, 1919
6. Returning home on S.S. *Olympia*, April, 1919

The Canadian Prime Minister, Sir Robert Borden, was in London attending sessions of the Imperial War Conference when he learned of the victory at Vimy and its cost. Greatly disturbed by the growing disparity between losses and voluntary enlistments, he returned to Canada determined to introduce a conscription bill and if possible form a coalition government to implement it. A period of intense political activity followed during which a Military Service Act was duly passed, a union government was formed under Borden's leadership but with Laurier refusing

to enter, and an election was called for December 17, 1917. The election gave the Union Government the strong mandate for conscription that it had sought but proved Laurier correct in his belief that the country had become dangerously divided — Unionists won only three of Quebec's 65 seats and lost only twenty of the remaining 170.

The Armistice ending the war was signed on November 11, 1918, after a last desperate and almost successful German offensive had been finally halted and rolled back. In the peace-making that followed at Versailles and

5

6

in the League of Nations which was one of the
outcomes, Borden insisted on a separate role
for Canada comparable to that he had won for
the Canadian Army overseas during the war.
Borden and the country as a whole had come a
long way since the pre-war debates on contributions to the Royal Navy. The trend
toward national autonomy was now clearly
marked.

48. THE TWENTIES. I, PROSPERITY

1. Streetcar on fire during Winnipeg General Strike, June 21, 1919
2. Troops on Main Street
3. Henry Wise Wood
4. Grenfell Mission (upper right), Battle Harbour, Newfoundland
5. Sir Frederick Banting
6. Imperial Oil Junkers "Rene" and "Vic" before attempted flight to Norman Wells, Feb. 1921
7. First well at Norman Wells.

8. Calgary during Turner Valley boom, 1914
9. Turner Valley after development in the twenties
10. Viscount Byng of Vimy
11. Arthur Meighen
12. Mackenzie King during 1926 election
13. Inaugural service of the United Church of Canada, June 10, 1925
14. Construction at Beauharnois power site

Anxiety and confusion, aggravated by the "red scare" that followed the Bolshevik Revolution in Russia, marked the period of immediate post-war readjustment. Rural discontent and distrust of either of the old parties led to the rise of a Progressive movement in the West and Ontario, its most outstanding leader being Henry Wise Wood of Alberta. Similar unrest within the less powerful and more frustrated industrial working class manifested itself in the form of flaring violence. The Winnipeg General Strike, the most important example of this, culminated on June 21, 1919, in rioting, the burning of a

10

11

12

13

14

streetcar, two deaths when the Royal North West Mounted Police fired on the crowd, and the calling out of the troops to restore order.

The troubles of 1919 were succeeded with surprising speed in the twenties by an atmosphere of economic confidence and optimistic idealism. Immigration was renewed on a large scale, crops were bountiful, and major industrial and power projects such as that at Beauharnois were commenced. Of particular interest were Imperial Oil's pioneering use of the aeroplane to open up the North and its successful development of Turner Valley's resources despite the earlier boom and bust of

1914. Pride could be taken too in Banting's discoveries connected with insulin and Grenfell's medical missions around the Newfoundland coast. The churches were strong and were strengthened by a union brought about in 1925 of the Methodists, Congregationalists, and the majority of the Presbyterians. Peace abroad seemed assured by the League of Nations and the Kellogg Pact, while at home greater political stability emerged strangely enough from the crisis of 1926 when Byng, having refused Mackenzie King request for dissolution of Parliament, granted one a few days later to his successor, Arthur Meighen. King's victory

in the election that followed, however embarrassing to the governor general, offered the first real hope since the conscription issue had been raised in 1917 for return to a workable system of party government.

Such at least was how Canadian affairs appeared on the surface in the twenties. Lurking beneath were social, economic, and political weaknesses—a Beauharnois Scandal for example—that would be revealed when the American stock market crashed in 1929 and the searing drought and depression of the thirties began.

48. THE TWENTIES.
II, THE MOVE TO THE CITIES AND OTHER CHANGES

1. Model T Ford
2. "The Jack Pine" by Tom Thomson, 1916
3. Victoria Street, Toronto, in 1926
4. Radio station CJOC, Lethbridge, 1929
5. Adelaide and Bay, Toronto, in 1923
6. Off the road in Muskoka, 1925
7. Thrills on the silent screen

In the twenties, Canada's urban population was still a minority, but it was becoming a bare minority as young people flocked into sprawling and cluttered towns and cities. For many the new way of life never fully took the place of the old. A nostalgia for the countryside, evident in the paintings of Tom Thomson and members of the controversial new Group of Seven, was stronger than the will to create a coherent and satisfying urban mode of living. Town planning took second place to a search for solace in holidays by lake and sea or in exploratory trips by car.

Cars along with movies and radio were already producing revolutionary changes in habits and outlook. In 1920, there were just over one quarter of a million passenger automobiles in Canada; by 1930, there were well over a million and many additional miles of paved and gravel road for their use. Individuals and families acquired independent mobility on a scale previously unknown. At the same time movies and radio added two entirely new dimensions to amusement and the diffusion of knowledge. Music both popular and classical, national and international news, styles, slang, and fads swept across Canada—often from the United States—and penetrated to all ranks of society. The old inward-looking sense of community became diluted and alongside it there grew an awareness of a wider, more diverse, and complex world.

5

6

7

1

2

3

49. DROUGHT AND DEPRESSION.
    I, ON THE PRAIRIES

1. Cattle bones, 1930
2. Drifted dust
3. Tracks in the dust
4. Destitute family from abandoned farm
5. Alberta 1936 one dollar prosperity certificate
6. Social Credit rally, Sept. 1936
7. William Aberhart
8. "Bennett buggy"

The Great Depression that followed the New York stock market crash in October and November 1929 had a disastrous effect on the whole of Canada. Trade was drastically cut, prices and wages were forced down, and unemployment reached appalling proportions. Hardest hit because of their dependence on wheat were the Prairie provinces. The price of wheat declined 57 per cent during 1930 as compared with an average decline of 30 per cent for Canada's seventeen major exports. By December 1932, it had fallen to 38 cents a bushel, the lowest point ever reached on the Winnipeg exchange.

When drought was added to depression,

the situation became catastrophic, especially in the arid Palliser Triangle of southern Alberta and Saskatchewan. Bones of cattle littered the plains almost like those of the buffalo fifty years before. Drifted dust clogged roads and swept around abandoned buildings. What had been prosperous farms and ranches in the twenties became in the thirties as deserted and desolate as the surface of the moon. About one quarter of Canada's farm acreage suffered successive crop failures between 1930 and 1937. The worst year was 1937, especially in Saskatchewan where two-thirds of the farm population was left completely destitute when field-crop yield totalled

6

7

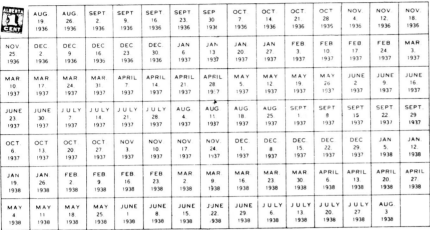

5

4

8

only $52,000,000 in gross value as compared $146,000,000 the year before and $300,000,000 in each of the three years before 1929.

The problem of relief was almost overwhelming because it involved the provision not only of food, clothing, shelter, and fuel, as in the case of the unemployed in industry, but also, year after year, of seed, fodder, and the various other requirements of farmers struggling back towards self-support. Governments at all levels and private charity did what could be done to help, and hard work and ingenious economies made up the rest — "Bennett Buggies" became the last resort of those unable to afford gas for their old flivers

or wagons to replace them. In Alberta "Bible Bill" Aberhart, founder of Calgary's Prophetic Bible Institute and widely popular for his religious broadcasts, took up C. H. Douglas's Social Credit theories, offered them as the solution to Alberta's problems, and became premier in 1935 when Social Crediters won 56 of the provincial legislature's 63 seats. An early Social Credit experiment was the issuance of prosperity certificates for circulation as substitute money. The sale of stamps to be attached each week by the current holders was intended to create a fund for their eventual redemption. They were issued mainly to pay for work on the highways, but

when banks and other businesses refused to honour them their use had to be discontinued. Other Social Credit legislation fared no better, being refused assent, disallowed, or declared unconstitutional by the courts. In practice, Aberhart's program soon became quite orthodox, even conservative, although declarations continued to be made that all that stood in the way of paying social dividends of $25 a month to each Albertan was the province's domination by the banks and other financial institutions controlled by Ottawa.

147

1

2

49. DROUGHT AND DEPRESSION.
II, UNEMPLOYMENT

1. The "March on Ottawa" of the unemployed, Calgary, 1935
2. Unemployed "marchers"
3. More "marchers"
4. Riot in Market Square, Regina, during "march," July 1, 1935
5. Building landing strips as relief project, Salmo, B.C., June, 1934
6. Relief camp at Hall's Lake, Ontario, 1934
7. "Soup kitchen," 1933
8. Meal in "soup kitchen," 1933

3

4

When unemployment reached its peak in 1933, over 800,000 Canadians out of a total labour force of 4,275,000 — about one out of every six — were in the frightening and humiliating position of being unable to find work to support themselves and whatever dependents they might have. The number had leapt upward from 371,000 in 1930 and only 65,000 in 1928; it would decline all too slowly until the outbreak of war in 1939. The problem was without precedent in Canadian history and was made more difficult to cope with by Canada's constitutional division of powers and revenues between the federal and the number of provincial governments.

Relief came traditionally within the sphere of the municipalities and therefore of the provinces to which these were responsible. The magnitude of the problem, however, and its differing impact from region to region — provinces most heavily hit were of course least able to help themselves — made federal intervention essential. This came hesitantly and was accompanied by continued insistence on the constitutional responsibility of the provinces. It took the form mainly of grants-in-aid to the provincial governments totalling eventually about 50 per cent of all relief expenditure but varying with need, from a high of 85 per cent in Saskatchewan to only 32 per cent in Ontario and 29 per cent in Quebec. Beginning in 1932, the federal government also set up relief camps for transients, providing them with food, shelter, and 20 cents a day in return for work on air strips and other public projects. When the lowest depths of the depression were reached the camps contained some 20,000 men.

The camps, the soup kitchens, and other public and private efforts could only achieve so much, and frustrations grew as years passed

5

6

7

8

and the economy seemed unable to turn the corner toward renewed prosperity. In British Columbia where the unusually rapid growth of the 'twenties had been succeeded by a slump of corresponding proportions, tensions became particularly great among a working class long known for its radicalism. In June 1935, 900 "relief strikers," as they called themselves, clambered aboard freight cars at Vancouver and other points in British Columbia and began a "march on Ottawa" to protest conditions in the camps. Others joined them as they moved eastward through Alberta and into Saskatchewan. At Regina, on June 14,

some 2000 were stopped and provided with temporary accommodation while their leaders were assisted on to Ottawa to meet with Prime Minister Bennett. Fruitless discussions were followed by their return to Regina and orders from the Prime Minister to the Royal North West Mounted Police to prevent the march from continuing eastward. On the evening of July 1, police intervention during a mass meeting in downtown Regina resulted in three hours of rioting during which a Regina police detective was beaten to death, the city police fired into the crowd (the Royal North West Mounted Police had gone into action with

purposely empty holsters), a number of injuries took place, and a number of arrests were made. Conciliatory action by the Saskatchewan Liberal government, not averse to making political capital out of Bennett's rigidity, persuaded the marchers to turn back westward again and the most serious threat to law and order during the depression was at an end.

1   2   3   4

50. PRE-WAR POLITICS

1. R. B. Bennett
2. J. S. Woodsworth
3. Ernest Lapointe
4. C. D. Howe
5. Mackenzie King and Walter Riddell at Geneva Conference, 1936
6. Their Majesties King George VI and Queen Elizabeth, Ottawa, May 19, 1939

5

Continuing unemployment was a major factor in the resounding defeat of R. B. Bennett in the election of 1935 and the restoration to office with an unprecedented majority of a Liberal government under Mackenzie King, a government that would remain in power throughout the coming war and well on into the post-war period. Important members were Ernest Lapointe, Laurier's successor as head of the French-Canadian wing of the party, and C. D. Howe who would soon play the major role in organizing Canada's economy for war. Elected to the House of Commons for the first time were seventeen Social Crediters, all

but two of them from Alberta, and seven members of the recently founded Co-operative Commonwealth Federation party dedicated to social reform under the remarkable leadership of J. S. Woodsworth.

Several significant changes in Canadian policy, especially with respect to tariffs and international politics, were to result from the change in government. Bennett's view of tariffs, and that of his party, had been that they should be used to protect Canadian producers and to force concessions from other countries —to blast a way into world markets. He had taken this line with some success during the

Ottawa Economic Conference of 1932 and by hard bargaining had obtained for Canada a larger share of the British market without yielding very much in return. Mackenzie King and the Liberals, on the other hand, favoured removing as many of the barriers to international trade as possible and cultivating, in particular, closer trade relations with the United States. Agreements that made substantial advances along these lines, which happened fortunately to coincide with the views of the American Secretary of State, Cordell Hull, were entered into in 1935 and were extended in 1937 and 1938.

6

Having become a member of the League of Nations at the time of its founding in 1919 and an autonomous nation within the British Commonwealth by the Statute of Westminster in 1931, Canada had an independent, if small, role to play in the disastrous course of events leading to the Second World War. Overshadowing all else when Mackenzie King became prime minister for the third time on October 23, 1935, was Italy's twenty-day-old invasion of Abyssinia. During earlier discussions in the League of Nations, designed to restrain Italy, the Bennett government had taken a strong stand in support of Britain's policy of sanctions. When their actual application was being discussed in October, Canada's permanent representative in Geneva, Walter Riddell, was unable to obtain instructions because of the government change-over taking place in Ottawa. He assumed that the new government would take the same line as the old and proposed inclusion of the vital sanction on oil. An ominous rift immediately became apparent in Canadian opinion. French Canadians were indifferent or a little inclined to sympathize with their fellow Roman Catholic and Latin people. Many of the English, influenced partly by Commonwealth loyalties, whose continuing strength would become abundantly evident during the magnificent Royal Visit of 1939, were firmly convinced that effective action by the League was necessary or collective security would be at an end. Mackenzie King, more sensitive to problems of Canadian unity than to international dangers, repudiated Riddell's initiative and himself argued at Geneva the following year that conciliation rather than force should be used in pursuing the League's objectives. War drew one step nearer.

51. THE SECOND WORLD WAR.
I, THE EARLY YEARS

1. Troopship leaving "an east coast port," 1939
2. Winter on the North Atlantic
3. Convoy assembled at Halifax
4. Depth charge exploding
5. Survivors of submarine sunk by H.M.C.S. *St. Thomas*, Jan. 1945
6. Tiger Moth trainers
7. Spitfires
8. Halifax bomber being loaded with high explosives and incendiaries
9. Dieppe, Aug. 19, 1942

The Second World War broke out when Hitler's invasion of Poland on September 1, 1939, provoked Britain and France to declare war two days later. On September 10, Canada made her own separate declaration and by December 17 Canadian troops were beginning to arrive in the United Kingdom. Some crossed into France briefly before that country's collapse but, except for this, the Canadian Army's lot for several years during which fighting centred in North Africa and on the Russian front was limited to garrison duty and training.

The Royal Canadian Navy entered the war with a complement of thirteen ships and about 1800 men—fewer in both categories than the losses it would suffer during the next five and a half years. Its first duty, to defend Canada's coastal waters against enemy surface raiders, submarines, and mines, was extended by 1941 to include a major part in the cold, wearying, and uncomfortable task, punctuated frequently by sudden danger, of escorting huge convoys of supplies and reinforcements across the North Atlantic. And when the time came for the landings in North Africa, Italy, and Normandy, Canadian destroyers, torpedo boats, and landing craft of all sorts and sizes saw action in those waters as well

Canada's role in the air war was a particu-

6

7

8

9

larly important one because it included not only the extensive fighter, bomber, and patrol activity of the Royal Canadian Air Force—whose fatal casualties totalled over 17,000, not far short of those of the Army—but also primary responsibility for the British Commonwealth Air Training Plan. This Plan, agreed upon in December 1939 and in effect until March 1945, led to the eventual creation in Canada of 97 flying schools and the training of over 131,000 aircrew personnel from the United Kingdom, Australia, and New Zealand as well as Canada.

After their years of waiting in Britain, units of the Canadian Army finally made con-

tact with the enemy during the controversial Dieppe Raid of August 19, 1942. This was undertaken along with other smaller commando-type raids as what seemed the only feasible means of satisfying, partially at least, the loud demands being made for a "second front" in Western Europe to relieve the intense German pressure on Russia. It was the first major amphibious operation of the war in Europe and the lessons learned from it were to prove of immense value in later landings, particularly those in Normandy. But the cost was high: of the 4963 Canadian soldiers who took part, 3367 became casualties, 907 being killed and 1946 captured.

1

4

3

5

2

51. THE SECOND WORLD WAR.
II, THE INVASION OF EUROPE

1. Tank of Three Rivers Regiment north of Ortona, Jan. 1944
2. Crossing to Normandy, June, 1944
3. Landing craft from H.M.C.S. *Prince David* heading for the beaches
4. "North Novas" going ashore at Bernières
5. On the beaches, D-Day, June 6, 1944
6. Major D. V. Currie (left with pistol) and surrendering Germans at St. Lambert-sur-Dives, Aug. 1944

7. General H. D. G. Crerar
8. Entering Germany
9. Bailey raft near Neuyen, Holland
10. The Quebec Conference, 1943

Sustained action on the part of the Canadian Army began when the First Division and First Army Tank Brigade joined other Allied units to invade Sicily in July 1943. After the occupation of that island had been completed, a strengthened Canadian force crossed to the Italian mainland and with the British and Americans began a long and bitter struggle northward, fighting a heavy battle at Ortona in December before going on to help breach the Adolf Hitler Line across the Liri Valley in May and the Gothic Line along the Foglia River in September.

Meanwhile, the long-awaited attack on Europe's west coast, approved under the code name Overlord at the Quebec Conference in August 1943, had finally been launched and Canadian units were among those landed on the Normandy beaches on D-Day, June 6, 1944. They had suffered casualties, though by no means on the Dieppe scale, as a result of underwater obstacles, other extensive fortifi-

cations, and fierce German resistance—only one of the *Prince David's* landing craft was to reach shore although most of the men somehow managed to do so.

The successful break-out from the beaches was followed by Canadian participation in the capture of Caen and heavy combat during a push southward. On July 23, with its numbers augmented by new units rushed across the Channel, the First Canadian Army became fully operational under the commander who would eventually lead it into Germany, General H. D. Crerar. Its first task was to help close at Falaise a gap in the trap being

shut on large German forces still in Normandy. In fierce August fighting to hold St. Lambert in the Falaise gap, Major Currie of the South Alberta Regiment won the V.C. and an enterprising photographer obtained one of the great action pictures of the war.

After Falaise, the Canadians turned northeastward on the left flank of the Allied advance clearing the Channel coast and moving on into Holland where a bloody amphibious struggle was needed to open the Scheldt estuary and the port of Antwerp to Allied shipping. When the war finally ended on May 7, 1945, the Canadian Army had crossed the frontier into

Germany. Its fatal casualties since D-Day numbered 10,833 and the total for the war 22,817—a heavy price to pay although dwarfed by the 59,544 of the First World War.

1 2

3

52. IN RECENT YEARS.
I, POLITICAL AND SOCIAL CHANGES

1. Ceremonies welcoming Newfoundland into Confederation, April 1, 1949. Front row, l. to r.: Prime Minister St. Laurent, Governor General Lord Alexander, Premier Joseph Smallwood, Mackenzie King

2. Governor General Massey and Prime Minister Diefenbaker, January, 1959

3. Dominion-Provincial Conference, July 1965. Front row, l. to r.: Jean Lesage (Quebec), Prime Minister Pearson, Governor General Vanier, John Robarts (Ontario); back row: Ross Thatcher (Saskatchewan), Louis Robichaud (New Brunswick), Walter Shaw (Prince Edward Island), Duff Roblin (Manitoba), Joseph Smallwood (Newfoundland), W. A. C. Bennett (British Columbia), Robert Stanfield (Nova Scotia), and Ernest Manning (Alberta)

4. Television rehearsal

5. Yorkville, Toronto

6. Avenue Road, Toronto

Despite tensions resulting from the "cold war" and from the rapidity of social and economic change, Canada became on the whole prosperous and self-confident within a very few years after the Second World War. The Liberal government, under Mackenzie King until 1948 and then under Louis St. Laurent, proved highly competent in making the necessary post-war adjustments, and capital flowed in for huge economic ventures. New construction changed the appearance of cities while a great wave of immigration swelled their population and altered in some respects their

4

5

6

character. In 1949, Newfoundland became Canada's tenth province, rounding out Confederation. In 1952, Vincent Massey became the first Canadian to be appointed Governor General. Later that same year Canadian television broadcasting began, opening up vast opportunities in the realms of entertainment and education along with incalculable possibilities of challenge to established social and cultural patterns.

An end to the long period of political stability came when John Diefenbaker toppled the St. Laurent government in 1957, was

himself overthrown two elections later in 1963, and was succeeded by Lester Pearson and a new Liberal government that remained in a minority even after another election in 1965. Political bickerings, frustrations, and a taint of corruption haunted the House of Commons under these circumstances, tending to discredit it with the public in a way reminiscent of the last years of Conservative rule before 1896 and of much of the longer period between the defeat of Laurier in 1911 and the victory of Mackenzie King in 1935. To a greater extent however than on those

previous occasions, the weaknesses of the government in Ottawa were of concern also because of their effect on the balance of power between the Dominion and the provinces, already shifting in the direction of the latter because of the greater emphasis being placed on education and social welfare and because of the revolutionary changes taking place in Quebec. Conferences of premiers, and at lower levels as well, began to evolve a new conception of federalism.

1

2

3

52. IN RECENT YEARS.
   II, ECONOMIC GROWTH AND CHANGE

1. Oil derrick in Alberta grain field
2. Laying a pipeline
3. Open pit iron mine at Steep Rock
4. St. Lawrence Seaway near Cornwall
5. Hydro development at Beechwood, N.B.
6. Potash bin at Esterhazy, Sask.

Economic growth in the years after the Second World War was particularly rapid. The Gross National Product — the total value of all goods and services produced — rose from $11,835 million in 1945 to $27,132 million in 1955 and $51,996 million in 1965. This resulted in part from rising prices but even in terms of constant dollars the increase was an impressive one.

The growth rate was not, of course, the same throughout the whole period. Indeed at the beginning, in the immediate post-war years, there was a slight decline while industry

was re-tooling for peacetime production. A gradual rise followed as war-deferred investment and consumer demand were taken care of and this continued at an accelerated rate when the Korean War began. The rate remained high in the mid-1950's with the undertaking of major construction projects such as the St. Lawrence Seaway, the transcontinental gas and pipelines, and the 350-mile railway to the iron ore deposits on the Quebec-Labrador border. A slackening of demand and greater international competition after 1957 led to a slowing down, but the rate

4

5

6

picked up again after 1961 as a result of new discoveries, technical innovations, large wheat sales to Russia and China, and a domestic market that was becoming of unprecedented importance owing to mounting standards of living as well as a rate of population growth almost equal to that of the first decade of the century — a 30 per cent increase from 14,009,000 in 1951 to 18,238,000 in 1961.

At the same time as the economy was expanding it was undergoing fundamental changes. Most rapid growth was in the category of electric power and gas utilities and in that of mining. Of particular importance were the iron ore of Steep Rock and on the Quebec-Labrador border, the oil of southern Alberta, the uranium of Beaverlodge Lake in Saskatchewan and Blind River in Ontario, the potash of Saskatchewan, and the aluminum refinery and neighbouring power development at Kitimat and Kemano respectively in British Columbia. Advances in connection with the old standbys of forestry, farming, fishing, and trapping were on the other hand well below average.

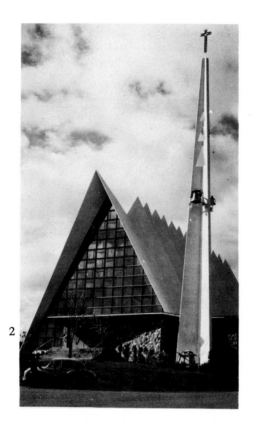

1

2

3

52. IN RECENT YEARS.
    III, A NEW OUTLOOK

1. Cloverleaf on Macdonald-Cartier Freeway
2. Eglise Saint-Marc, Bagotville
3. Unloading supplies at Yellowknife
4. Radar station at Great Whale River, Quebec
5. Northern Transportation Company truck and driver

In a period of obviously rapid change, it was not surprising that Canadians were acquiring a new outlook with respect to themselves and their country as the hundredth anniversary of Confederation approached. To a considerable extent this was part of the shift in viewpoint taking place in North America generally and in other parts of the world as affluence increased and the impact was fully felt of the automobile, the aeroplane, the television set, the computer, and the countless other scientific and technological developments that were transforming daily living and erasing former barriers to thought or action.

In Canada as elsewhere in these circumstances, and even in what had until recently been a rather isolated and conservative French Canada, the trend was toward freedom and flexibility — or sometimes just the new and the different — whether in architecture or hair style, manners or morals, educational processes or social organization, party leadership or constitutional framework. The old ways, and frequently the old men, were no longer acceptable.

There was as well, of course, a distinctively Canadian element in Canada's reaction to the 1960's arising out of her special circumstances

4

5

— her federalism, her French-English dualism, her historical associations with the United Kingdom and her geographical proximity to the United States. Canadians were highly conscious — perhaps in the long run overly conscious — of all of these, of how they divided Canadian opinion, and of the danger that in a world accustomed to change one or another might become a threat to the national entity. There was a corresponding tendency perhaps to overlook the extent to which the vast improvements being made in communications and transportation were serving to broaden out Canada to the northward and bind her together into the sort of great transcontinental unit that had long before been the dream of the fur trader.

COVER. top, National Museum of Canada; bottom, National Aeronautics and Space Administration, Washington, D.C.

p. ii. ("The Clearing," by Jacques de Tonnancour) The National Gallery of Canada, Ottawa

1. 1, 2, 3, 4, National Museum of Canada; 5, *A Historical Atlas of Canada* (Toronto: Nelson, 1960)

2. 1, Public Archives of Canada (hereafter P.A.C.); 2, Canadian National; 3, National Film Board; 4, *Historical Atlas of Canada*; 5, Royal Ontario Museum; 6, National Film Board

3. 1, 2, Traquair Collection, McGill University (hereafter Traquair); 3, Edgar Davidson; 4, 5, P.A.C.

4. 1, National Museum of Canada; 2, P.A.C.; 3, Notman Collection, McGill University (hereafter Notman); 4, 5, P.A.C.; 6, John Macfie.

5. 1, 2, Edgar Davidson; 3, P.A.C.; 4, Edgar Davidson; 5, Wilfred Jury

6. 1, P.A.C.; 2, Notman; 3, Traquair; 4, 5, 6, Traquair; 7, Congrégation de Notre Dame, Montréal

7I. 1, P.A.C.; 2, 3, Inventaire des Oeuvres d'art, Québec; 4, P.A.C.; 5, Inventaire des Oeuvres d'art, Québec; 6, P.A.C.

7II. 1, National Gallery of Canada, Ottawa; 2, Canadian National; 3, Inventaire des Oeuvres d'art, Québec; 4, Canadian National 5, P.A.C.; 6, The National Gallery of Canada, Ottawa; 7, Traquair; 8, Canadian National

8. 1, Hudson's Bay Company; 2, New Brunswick Museum; 3, 4, 5, P.A.C.; 6, Notman; 7, National Film Board; 8, Inventaire des Oeuvres d'art, Québec

9. 1, 2, P.A.C.; 3, McCord Museum, McGill University; 4, 5, 6, P.A.C.; 7, The National Gallery of Canada, Ottawa

10. 1, P.A.C.; 2, The National Gallery of Canada, Ottawa

11. 1, P.A.C.; 2, The National Gallery of Canada, Ottawa; 3, 4, 5, P.A.C.; 6, Edgar Davidson

12. 1, 2, Toronto Public Libraries; 3, Nova Scotia Information Service; 4, 5, Traquair; 6, P.A.C.; 7, Ontario Archives; 8, Ontario Government

13I. 1, P.A.C.; 2, McCord Museum, McGill University; 3, The National Gallery of Canada, Ottawa; 4, Hudson's Bay Company; 5, P.A.C.; 6, Ontario Archives; 7, Hudson's Bay Company

13II. 1, P.A.C.; 2, Edgar Davidson; 3, P.A.C.; 4, Glenbow Foundation; 5, National Museum of Canada; 6, National Gallery of Canada

14. 1, Royal Ontario Museum; 2, Edgar Collard; 3, 4, P.A.C.; 5, 6, Toronto Public Libraries

15. 1, New Brunswick Travel Bureau; 2, Ontario Government; 3, Toronto Public Libraries; 4, Canadian National; 5, 6, P.A.C.

16. 1, P.A.C.; 2, 3, Ontario Archives; 4, Toronto Public Libraries; 5, 6, 7, Molson Archives

17. 1, 2, Toronto Public Libraries; 3, University of Western Ontario; 4, P.A.C.; 5, Toronto Public Libraries

18. 1, P.A.C.; 2, 3, 4, New Brunswick Museum

19. 1, 2, Nova Scotia Information Service; 3, 4, Traquair; 5, Ontario Government; 6, McCord Museum, McGill University; 7, Ontario Government; 8, New Brunswick Government

20. 1, Traquair; 2, Inventaire des Oeuvres d'art, Québec; 3, 4, P.A.C.; 5, 6, Toronto Public Libraries

21. 1, Edgar Davidson; 2, 4, P.A.C.; 3, Notman; 5, Ontario Archives; 6, 7, 8, P.A.C.; 9, Quebec Government; 10, University of Toronto Library

22. 1, 2, Notman; 3, 4, 5, Canadian National; 6, Ralph Greenhill

23. 1, Notman; 2, 3, P.A.C.; 4, Ontario Archives; 5, 6, P.A.C.; 7, Ontario Government; 8, Ralph Greenhill

24. 1, Ralph Greenhill; 2, Toronto Public Libraries; 3, The National Gallery of Canada, Ottawa; 4, 5, 6, Toronto Public Libraries; 7, P.A.C.

25. 1, P.A.C.; 2, 3, Edgar Davidson; 4, 5, P.A.C.; 6, Hudson's Bay Company; 7, P.A.C.; 8, 9, Hudson's Bay Company

26. 1, National Gallery of Canada, Ottawa; 2, Edgar Davidson; 3, 4, P.A.C.; 5, Glenbow Foundation

27. 1, P.A.C.; 2, 3, 4, Manitoba Archives; 5, 6, 7, 8, P.A.C.

28I. Miller Services (H. Pollard); 2, National Museum of Canada; 3, Provincial Archives, Victoria; 4, Hudson's Bay Company; 5, City Archives, Vancouver; 6, Provincial Archives, Victoria; 7, Canadian Pacific; 8, Glenbow Foundation; 9, Provincial Archives, Victoria

28II. 1, 2, 3, 4, Provincial Archives, Victoria; 5, City Archives, Vancouver

29. 1, 2, 3, P.A.C.; 4, Ontario Archives; 5, 6, P.A.C.

30I. 1, 2, P.A.C.; 3, Toronto Public Libraries

30II. 1, P.A.C.; 2, Notman; 3, 4, P.A.C.; 5, 6, 7, 8, 9, Notman

31. 1, P.A.C.; 2, 3, Manitoba Archives; 4, P.A.C.; 5, Ontario Archives; 6, Manitoba Archives; 7, 8, P.A.C.

32I. 1, Provincial Archives, Victoria; 2, City Archives, Vancouver; 3, Geological Survey of Canada; 4, Glenbow Foundation

32II. 1, Canadian National; 2, P.A.C.; 3, 4, Canadian National

33. 1, Provincial Archives, Victoria; 2, 3, P.A.C.; 4, 5, Glenbow Foundation; 6, P.A.C.

34. 1, 2, P.A.C.; 3, The National Gallery of Canada, Ottawa; 4, P.A.C.; 5, University of Western Ontario

35. 1, Geological Survey of Canada; 2, 3, Notman; 4, Glenbow Foundation; 5, 6, Geological Survey of Canada; 7, Notman

36. 1, P.A.C.; 2, Glenbow Foundation; 3, P.A.C.; 4, Archives of Saskatchewan; 5, 6, 7, 8, Glenbow Foundation; 9, Archives of Saskatchewan; 10, Canadian Pacific

37. 1, Notman; 2, Provincial Archives, Victoria; 3, City Archives, Vancouver; 4, Glenbow Foundation; 5, P.A.C.; 6, Ontario Archives; 7, Notman; 8, 9, Canadian Pacific; 10, Glenbow Foundation; 11, P.A.C.; 12, Toronto Public Libraries

38I. 1, 2, Glenbow Foundation; 3, 4, City Archives, Vancouver; 5, Glenbow Foundation

38II. 1, Notman; 2, City Archives, Vancouver; 3, 4, Notman

38III. 1, 2, Ontario Archives; 3, 4, Canadian Pacific; 5, P.A.C.; 6, Glenbow Foundation; 7, Archives of Saskatchewan; 8, 9, Notman

39I. 1, P.A.C.; 2, Canadian Pacific; 3,

SOURCES

P.A.C.; 4, Glenbow Foundation; 5, Canadian Pacific

39II.1, Manitoba Archives; 2, 3, 4, 5, 6, 7, 8, 9, P.A.C.

39III. 1, Canadian Pacific; 2, P.A.C.; 3, 4, Canadian Pacific; 5, 6, 7, Glenbow Foundation; 8, Manitoba Archives

40I. 1, P.A.C.; 2, Glenbow Foundation; 3, Manitoba Archives; 4, Glenbow Foundation; 5, P.A.C.; 6, Archives of Saskatchewan

40II. 1, 2, P.A.C.; 3, Archives of Saskatchewan; 4, 5, 6, 7, P.A.C.; 8, Archives of Saskatchewan

40III. 1, 2, Archives of Saskatchewan; 3, Glenbow Foundation; 4, Archives of Saskatchewan; 5, Notman; 6, P.A.C.; 7, 8, 9, 10, 11, Glenbow Foundation

40IV. 1, P.A.C.; 2, Manitoba Archives; 3, Glenbow Foundation; 4, Manitoba Archives; 5, 6, P.A.C.; 7, National Grain Company, Winnipeg; background, P.A.C.

40V. 1, 2, Glenbow Foundation; 3, Archives of Saskatchewan; 4, 5, P.A.C.

40VI. 1, Canadian National; 2, 3, P.A.C.; 4, 5, 6, Glenbow Foundation; 7, 8, Notman

41I. 1, 2, Provincial Archives, Victoria; 3, P.A.C.

41II. 1, Provincial Archives, Victoria; 2, Glenbow Foundation; 3, 4, Public Archives of Canada; 5, Provincial Archives, Victoria; 6, 7, City Archives, Vancouver

42. 1, Glenbow Foundation; 2, Nova Scotia Information Service; 3, 4, Bell Telephone Company of Canada, Dr. Melville Bell Grosvenor, and the National Geographic Society; 5, Notman; 6, P.A.C.; 7, Notman; 8, 9, P.A.C.; 10, National Film Board.

43I. 1, 2, McCord Museum, McGill University; 3, 4, Notman; 5, P.A.C; 6, Notman

43II. 1, P.A.C.; 2, 3, 4, Notman

43III. I, 2, Imperial Oil; 3, *London Free Press*; 4, Imperial Oil; 5, *London Free Press*; 6, Notman; 7, P.A.C.; 8, *London Free Press*

43IV. 1, 2, 3, Notman; 4, 5, Geological Survey of Canada; 6, Notman

43V. 1, 2, 3, 4, 5, 6, 7, 8, Notman

43VI. 1, Toronto Public Libraries; 2, The T. Eaton Company; 3, 4, 5, 6, Toronto Public Libraries

44I. 1, Miller Services (H. Pollard); 2, Glenbow Foundation; 3, 4, 5, P.A.C.

44II. 1, P.A.C.; 2, Victorian Order of Nurses; 3, P.A.C.*; 4, 5, Notman; 6, National Museum of Canada; 7, 8, Glenbow Foundation; 9, National Museum of Canada

44III. 1, McCord Museum, McGill University; 2, 3, 4, 5, 6, P.A.C.

45. 1, 2, 3, 4, P.A.C.; 5, Ministère des Affaires culturelles du Québec; 6, 7, P.A.C.; 8, Ontario Archives; 9, Archives of Saskatchewan; 10, 11, 12, 13, 14, P.A.C.

46. 1, 2, P.A.C.; 3 Glenbow Foundation; 4, 5, 6, 7, 8, 9, P.A.C.; 10, 11, Department of National Defence

47I. 1, Glenbow Foundation; 2, P.A.C.; 3, Canadian Pacific; 4, 5, P.A.C.; 6, Department of National Defence; 7, 8, 9, 10, P.A.C.

47II. 1, 2, 3, 4, 5, 6, 7, 8, 9, 10, 11, 12, 13, P.A.C.

47III. 1, 2, 3, 4, 5, 6, 7,* 8, 9, 10, 11, 12, P.A.C.

47IV. 1, 2, 3, 4, 5, 6, P.A.C.

48I. A. E. Foote, Winnipeg; 2, Manitoba Archives; 3, Glenbow Foundation; 4, Not-man; 5, P.A.C.; 6, Imperial Oil; 7, Glenbow Foundation; 8, Imperial Oil; 9, Glenbow Foundation; 10, 11, 12, P.A.C.; 13, United Church Archives; 14, P.A.C.

48II. 1, Glenbow Foundation; 2, National Gallery of Canada; 3, Miller Services; 4, Glenbow Foundation; 5, 6, 7, Miller Services

49I. 1, Archives of Saskatchewan; 2, 3, Manitoba Archives; 4, Glenbow Foundation; 5, P.A.C.; 6, Glenbow Foundation; 7, P.A.C.; 8, Manitoba Archives

49II. 1, 2, Archives of Saskatchewan; 3, *Toronto Star*; 4, Archives of Saskatchewan; 5, P.A.C; 6, Ontario Archives; 7, 8, Glenbow Foundation

50. 1, 2, 3, 4, 5, 6, P.A.C.

51I. 1, P.A.C.; 2, 3, 4, 5, 6, 7, 8, Department of National Defence; 9, P.A.C.

51II. 1, 2, 3, 4, 5, 6, 7, 8, 9, Department of National Defence; 10, P.A.C.

52I. 1, Newton Studios, Ottawa; 2, Miller Services; 3, Dominion-Wide Photographs, Ottawa; 4, National Film Board; 5, 6, Miller Services.

52II. 1, National Film Board; 2, Imperial Oil; 3, 4, National Film Board; 5, New Brunswick Travel Bureau; 6, Saskatchewan government.

52III. 1, National Film Board; 2, Inventaire des Oeuvres d'Art, Québec; 3, 4, 5, National Film Board.

p. 162 ("Le Visiteur du soir," by J. P. Lemieux) The National Gallery of Canada, Ottawa

*It was unfortunately not possible to trace the ownership of this photograph.